Fifty Songs
for High Voice

EDVARD GRIEG
(1843–1907)

Fifty Songs
for High Voice

DOVER PUBLICATIONS, INC.
Mineola, New York

Bibliographical Note

This Dover edition, first published in 2005, is an unabridged republication of
the work as originally published by Oliver Ditson Co., Boston, in 1908.

International Standard Book Number: 0-486-44130-X

Manufactured in the United States of America
Dover Publications, Inc., 31 East 2nd Street, Mineola, N.Y. 11501

CONTENTS

INDEX

EDVARD GRIEG

THERE is an expression, "I bought it for a song," which implies that a song is a mere trifle, a thing of little value. Now, it cannot be denied that the songs of the great masters, from Bach and Handel to Beethoven, are indeed for the most part mere trifles compared with the best numbers in their oratorios and symphonies. Schubert was the first great master who infused as much genius into his songs as into his symphonies or sonatas; and others, fortunately, soon followed his example. Among these, Edvard Grieg is conspicuous. His songs contain the very quintessence of his genius,—a world of musical thought, fancy, emotion; a lavish abundance of fresh melody, novel harmony, ravishing modulation, enchanting tone-color. They are entirely original,—as different from the songs of other countries as the scenery of Norway is from the scenery of Germany, France, and Italy. To sing them is like making an excursion in the Northern fjords.

Strange to say, most of these enchanting songs are still unknown, to professionals as well as amateurs; they are buried treasures, music of the future. One often reads that "every school-girl plays and sings Grieg;" but that is an absurd exaggeration. Grieg's friend, the Norwegian composer Schjelderup, came nearer the truth when he said: "A few of the 'famous' songs are sung interminably, and that is about all. Who knows Grieg's settings of the poems by Ibsen, Vinje, and Garborg, which are among his best?"

It is the object of the present volume to change this deplorable state of affairs by making the best fifty of Grieg's one hundred and thirty-five songs conveniently accessible in an English version, and at the same time supplying such information as seems essential for a thorough comprehension and interpretation of them. A few years ago the eminent violinist Johannes Wolf, who made concert tours with Grieg in England and on the Continent, wrote to the editor of this volume: "His works are full of passion and poetry; the more I play them, the more I love them; always I find freshness and beauty. But," he adds, "few know how to play Grieg." To do that, "one must know him, his beautiful country, and the Norwegian character." This is emphatically true. Not that it is necessary to be a Scandinavian to do justice to Grieg's music. He himself wrote, a few months before his death, that the best exponent of his art was an Australian. But every singer or player of his works ought to know something of his life, his ideals, and the quaint customs and picturesque scenery which colored and gave shape to his music.

While Edvard Grieg was born in Norway (at Bergen, on June 15, 1843), his great-grandfather was a Scotchman,—a merchant who wrote his name Greig and was probably related to General Greigh. After the battle of Culloden, in 1746, which was so disastrous to the Scotch, he emigrated to Norway, where he changed his name to Grieg (to ensure the correct pronunciation), and married a Norwegian. Their son, John, who occupied the post of British consul at Bergen, also married a Norwegian, and so did his son, Alexander, the father of the composer, who thus had much more Norwegian than Scotch blood in his veins. His musical talent came to him entirely from the Norwegian side; he inherited his gifts from his mother (Gesine Hagerup), who played the piano sufficiently well to appear at public concerts. She had weekly soirées at her house at which Edvard heard much good music, especially by Mozart and Weber, his mother's favorite composers. She also gave him piano lessons, and at the age of twelve he wrote his first composition, a set of variations on a German melody. He took this to school and showed it to his teacher, who, however, pulled his hair and told him not to waste his time on such foolishness!

Edvard's father never cared much more for

his music than that teacher did, even after he had made his mark. But he influenced him favorably otherwise, for he was a man of character and culture. He took Edvard, when a lad of fifteen, on a trip to the mountains, on which occasion the grandeur of the Norwegian scenery made such a deep impression on the boy that he wanted to become a painter. He admired particularly the snowy solitudes, the precipitous cliffs, the glaciers, the thundering waterfalls. Luckily, at this crisis, the eminent violinist Ole Bull came to the rescue of music. He had often visited the Griegs and had promptly discovered the boy's talent. He advised the parents to send their son to Leipzig, and they followed his suggestion without a moment's hesitation, as they had themselves reached the conclusion that he was destined to be a musician.

Grieg entered the Leipzig Conservatory with joyous expectations and a vague idea that his mere presence there would soon make him a finished musician. He was displeased when he found that he was expected to do a great deal of work, and much of it pure drudgery. He was by no means a model student; much of his time was spent in dawdling and dreaming. But it was not all his fault. Many of the lessons given were unnecessarily dry and pedantic, and he was asked to compose chamber music and orchestral works before he had learned to handle his tools. What annoyed him particularly was the ultra-conservative attitude of most of the professors. Chopin and Wagner, whom he adored, were "forbidden fruit;" to some extent the same was true even of Schumann, one of the founders of the Conservatory. These things discouraged him, and for a time he neglected his work. But a reaction came. Seeing how industrious his classmates were (among them several young Englishmen who subsequently became famous: Arthur Sullivan, Edward Dannreuther, Franklin Taylor, and Walter Bache), he bestirred himself and went to the other extreme, the consequence being that in 1860 he broke down. Pleurisy supervened and left the young man to spend the remaining forty-seven years of his life with only one lung.

His mother came and took him home, but subsequently he returned and finished his studies at the Conservatory, passing the examinations successfully.

From Leipzig he went to Denmark, where he began to compose industriously, partly under the guidance of the famous composer Gade. But there was a still stronger influence and incitement to work. In 1864 he became engaged to his cousin Nina Hagerup, but for three long years he had to work hard to command sufficient income to marry her. It was largely owing to his betrothed that his genius assumed such a strong bent toward lyric song. For her he composed the best known of all his songs, *I Love Thee*, and many of his other gems.

Had Grieg remained in Germany he would still have become a great composer; but his songs and pieces would have lacked that exotic fragrance which constitutes one of their greatest charms. His *I Love Thee* illustrates this point. It is quite German; Schumann might have written it when at his best, for it is quite in his style; but Schumann could never have written *The First Primrose, The Swan, The Old Mother, On the Journey Home, At the Brookside, Minstrel's Song, The Mountain Maid, At Mother's Grave, From Monte Pincio*. These, and many others of the songs, only a *Norwegian* could have written, and only *one* Norwegian,—Edvard Grieg.

From Denmark Grieg passed on to his native country. For eight years he made Christiania his home, giving concerts and trying hard to educate the musical taste of his fellow citizens. For his compositions there was at this time very little demand. "He writes music that nobody wants to hear," the mother of the girl he was engaged to used to say. Consequently he had to make his living by teaching, conducting, and playing the organ in churches.

The first to discover his genius was Liszt. He had accidentally come across Grieg's first sonata for piano and violin, and was so much pleased that he wrote him a letter praising it for the inventive talent manifested in it. An important result of this letter was that the Norwegian Government granted him a sum of money which enabled him to go to Rome and visit Liszt. For his own very interesting account of his intercourse the reader must be referred to the editor's *Grieg and His Music* (John Lane Co.). Liszt was enthusiastic over Grieg's pieces, especially the piano concerto, and his final admonition was one which often upheld Grieg in later years when the bold originality of his music made it the target of critical arrows: "Keep steadily on; I tell you, you have the gifts, and—*do not let them intimidate you!*"

Schubert once said that creative artists should be supported by the government—an opinion which Wagner echoed. The Norwegian Government began long ago to do that very thing. Grieg, in 1874, received an annuity of sixteen hundred crowns (four hundred and forty dollars), which—as the expenses of living in Norway were low—enabled him to give up teaching and devote more time to composing. He made his home in Bergen again, and there wrote, among other things, at Ibsen's special request, the incidental music to *Peer Gynt*, which, in the form of suites, is to this day among the most popular concert pieces. In 1877 he made his residence at Lofthus, on the South Fjord, where he remained eight years, devoting most of his time to composing, varying this by making an occasional concert tour. But Lofthus, with all its scenic charms, had the disadvantage of being too much exposed to casual visitors and intruders, wherefore he moved, in 1885, to the villa Troldhaugen, near the railway station Hop, about five miles from Bergen, and this remained his home to the end of his life.

A simple life it was, the only sensational incident in it having been an occurrence in Paris which at the same time reveals his character in a most agreeable light. At the time of the Dreyfus trial the eminent orchestral conductor Edouard Colonne invited him to participate in a concert at the Châtelet Theatre. But Grieg replied that he was too indignant at the contempt for justice shown in France to enter into relations at that moment with the French public. It was an unwise answer. A writer in *Le Figaro* had said

not long before that among the most famous musicians of the time he knew none whose popularity in France equalled Grieg's. This popularity he risked losing; for had not Wagner's operas been boycotted in Paris many years because he had, in his play, *A Capitulation*, lampooned the French? But Grieg did not care. He had the courage, four years later, to accept Colonne's renewed invitation, and the chauvinists did not neglect the opportunity to hiss and to cry: "Apologize, you have insulted France!" The audience, however, took his part, and the result was an ovation, mingled with hisses.

This was the first time in his life—he was sixty years old—that he had ever been hissed. But he looked at the matter from a humorous point of view, writing to a friend: "I have seen much, but never such a comedy as that in the Châtelet Theatre on the nineteenth. But—who can tell?—if I had not been hissed I would perhaps not have had such an enormous success!"

His capacity for seeing the funny side of things is frequently shown in his letters, and it serves as a counterpart to his *Humoresken* for pianoforte. When his friend Oscar Meyer, the song writer, congratulated him on his election as a member of the French Legion of Honor, he replied: "My election is an 'honor' I share with 'legions,' so let us not waste more words about it."

He received many tempting offers for an American tour, but distrust of his health and aversion to the turbulent ocean made him refuse them all. To an American visitor who urged him to cross, he remarked that he would do so if he could get a guaranty that the Atlantic would behave itself; "but," he added, "it must be a written guaranty!"

In European countries he gave a few concerts nearly every year, and the house was always sold out weeks in advance. He was a conductor who could get "nervous thrilling bursts and charming sentiment" out of any good orchestra, and he was a first-class pianist, playing his own pieces now with the wild abandon of Norwegian dancing peasants, now with the exquisite delicacy and refinement of a man of genius who fathoms the deepest secrets of the soul.

Personally he was as shy and delicate as some of his melodies. In December, 1906, he wrote to Oscar Meyer: "You are perfectly right in being astonished that I still give concerts. The fact is, however, that I allow myself to be persuaded to do so; I have, unfortunately, not strength of character enough to refuse. To appear in public is, to me, the most hateful thing I can imagine. And yet, to hear my works excellently performed and in accordance with my own interpretation — this is a thing I cannot resist."

This was three years after his sixtieth birthday. That birthday was celebrated all over Scandinavia and in other countries, especially in Germany, where many music lovers feel toward Grieg much as they do toward the equally modest and melodious Schubert. The German Emperor is particularly fond of Grieg's music, which reminds him of the picturesque Norwegian fjords he visits nearly every summer on the *Hohenzollern*. Once he entertained Grieg on this yacht, and during this visit an incident occurred to which the composer often referred with special pleasure. A strong and cold wind was blowing, and the Emperor, knowing of Grieg's delicate state of health, lent him his military cloak. As the composer was walking up and down the deck alone, an officer said to him: "Take care! His Majesty's mantle is dragging." At that moment the Kaiser returned and said with a smile: "The main thing is that our master must not catch cold."

The Kaiser was also one of the chief mourners when Grieg died, at Bergen, on September 4, 1907, after lying ill for a week in the hospital. To the widow he sent this dispatch: "I communicate to you, on your husband's death, my most cordial sympathy. He and his art will never be forgotten by me, nor by his compatriots, nor by the Germans. May God console you in your grief. I have charged my Ambassador to represent me at the funeral ceremony and to lay on his bier a wreath in my name."

Bergen solicited the honor of taking charge of the funeral services, but the Norwegian Government intervened and made it a national affair. More than forty thousand persons participated; all schools, shops, and factories were closed. Grieg's wish, expressed in 1894, that the funeral march he had written on the death of his friend Nordraak should be played at his own obsequies was fulfilled. As the procession marched along the streets past the houses draped in black, all the men bared their heads — for every Norwegian loves Grieg as if he were a member of his own family; and to this love is added pride and gratitude — for what other man had done more to make Norway known and admired by the world? In the words of Björnson: "He brought it about that Norwegian moods and Norwegian life are at home in every music room in the whole world."

Grieg's body was cremated, and in April, 1908, the ashes were deposited in a spot as romantic and moody as his music. From the villa Troldhaugen, which was his home during the last twenty years of his life, there is visible a promontory projecting into the fjord. At the extreme end of this there is a rock with a natural grotto. This grotto is not accessible by land, but can be reached only by boat, and the rock rises steep above it. Here the urn containing Grieg's ashes was deposited, and the grotto then closed forever and marked with an epitaph on a marble tablet indicating the former entrance.

The Northland Spirit in Music

A German critic once expressed his regret that Grieg " stuck in the fjord and never got out of it." Most music lovers are, on the contrary, delighted that his music is, like his life, — and now his ashes, — inseparable from the fjord. He began his career by writing German music; the first dozen or so of his songs were composed under the influence of Schubert and Schumann. Then came the Danish episode already referred to. Gade, the Dane, helped to arouse his musical ambition, but did not awaken his patriotic Scandinavian sentiment, being too much of a Germanist himself. He actually objected to the strong national color in the second violin sonata.

"Dear Grieg," he said, "your next sonata you really must make less Norwegian." But Grieg retorted boldly: "On the contrary, Professor, the next shall be more so!"

The courage of his convictions had come to him partly spontaneously, partly through the influence of two friends, Richard Nordraak and Ole Bull. Both were ardent patriots, convinced that musically Norway had something of great charm and eternal value to offer the world. Nordraak was a young enthusiast, a gifted composer, with whom Grieg played and discussed politics and nationalism. He died too young to make his mark. Ole Bull, in Grieg's youth, used to take him along on his tours to the mountainous interior, where they listened delightedly to the national airs as played by peasant fiddlers on their antique "fele." Then the great violinist transferred these wild airs, and played them, not only for the Griegs and the other Norwegians, but the world over, arousing unbounded enthusiasm.

The belief is still widely prevalent that Grieg did little more than Ole Bull—that he was simply a collector of national airs which he made accessible to the outside world, after dressing them up in appropriate harmonies. Several of his collections of pianoforte pieces (op. 17, 35, 66, 72) and a few other works are indeed based on borrowed melodies; but these constitute only a very small fraction of his productions; all the others are his own absolutely. Of his one hundred and thirty-five songs only one, *Solvejg's Song*, is based on a folk-tune. Grieg did not need to borrow tunes, for his own melodic faculty was astonishingly fertile. Norse folk-songs are noted for their freshness and beauty, yet, as Philip Hale has aptly remarked, "Look over these folk-songs, and see how superior to them in haunting beauty are the melodies of Grieg."

Grieg's strength, as Professor Niecks of Edinburgh University has remarked, "lies in the freshness and novelty of his ideas." This creat-

ing of "fresh and novel ideas" is the one thing in music which cannot be learned or taught. It is that which distinguishes genius from mere talent; and this we must bear in mind in determining Grieg's place among the masters. In point of originality he ranks with the greatest of them in all the elements of his art,—melody, harmony, modulation, rhythm, and coloring. His music is as unmistakably his own as his face.

While thus emphasizing his originality, we must bear in mind that he was nevertheless, like all other composers, subject to diverse influences. The masters who specially helped to mould his mind are Schubert, Schumann, Chopin, Liszt, and Wagner. Great and salutary, also, was the influence on him of the folk-music of Norway; it helped to make his own music racy of the soil, as the folk-music of Poland did that of Chopin, the folk-music of Bohemia that of Dvořák, the folk-music of Hungary that of Liszt. Like a tree with its roots in the soil of his native country, Grieg absorbed the chemical qualities of the Norwegian soil without losing any of his individuality.

The folk-music of Norway is more exotic—more "foreign" to our ears—than that of the other Scandinavian countries—Sweden and Denmark. It is peculiarly robust, often rugged as the bold rocks that overhang those narrow and winding arms of the sea which are called fjords. It delights in abrupt changes; its rhythms are irregular and capricious, the tonality uncertain and vacillating; and there is a preference for the minor mode and for quaint melodic intervals. Grieg himself, in speaking of the Norwegian peasant tunes, refers to their "blending of delicacy and grace with rough power and untamed wildness as regards their melody, and more particularly the rhythm." This blend we find in many of his own pieces, too; we find in them also the love of a drone bass changeless through many bars, the rhapsodic manner, the need of an ever changing *rubato* pace, which characterize Norse music.[1]

[1] *For details regarding the characteristics of Norwegian music the reader must be referred to the author's biography of Grieg, chapter viii. Before the appearance of this book the opinion previously referred to—that Grieg did little more than transplant*

(cont.)

Norwegian music differs from the Danish and Swedish very much as the scenery does. As I have said elsewhere: "The Norwegian is bolder, rougher, wilder, grander, yet with a green, fertile vale here and there in which strawberries and cherries reach a fragrance and flavor hardly attained anywhere else in the world." These green vales with luscious fruits are one of the main characteristics of Grieg's music. They impart a feeling of delight like that which overcomes a tourist going down a Swiss pass from the snowy Alps to the fig trees and vineyards of Italy.

Carl Engel, who made a special study of the varieties of national song, has tersely characterized the general spirit of Norwegian music. "It is a curious fact," he says, "that those nations which possess the most lugubrious music possess also the most hilarious tunes. The songs of the Norwegians are generally very plaintive, though at the same time very beautiful; and some of the Norwegian dances have perhaps more resemblance to dirges than to the dances of some other nations; but in single instances the Norwegian tunes exhibit an unbounded joy and cheerfulness, such as we rarely meet with in the music of other people. Indeed, the Norwegians, so far as their music is concerned, might be compared to the hypochondriac who occasionally, though but seldom, gives himself up to an almost excessive merriment."

Grieg himself, in a letter to the editor, wrote: "The fundamental trait of Norwegian folk-song as contrasted with the German is a deep melancholy, which may suddenly change to a wild unrestrained gayety. Mysterious gloom and indomitable wildness—these are the contrasts of Norwegian folk-song."

The Songs of Grieg

Beethoven is greatest in his adagios, and Dr. Dvořák once quoted approvingly to the editor of this volume the remark of Hans Richter that in the case of composers in general their slow movements are the supreme test and manifestation of genius. Schubert once wrote in his diary: "Grief sharpens the intellect and strengthens the soul, whereas joy seldom does anything for the one and makes the other weak or frivolous." On another page he wrote: "My musical compositions are the product of my intellect and my sorrows; those which were born of sorrow alone, appear to give the world the most satisfaction."

In looking over the Grieg songs we find a preponderance of those in which he gives expression to his own sorrows and those of the bards whose poems he set. Yet there are also not a few in which is embodied that "unbounded joy and cheerfulness" characteristic of the Norwegians—contrasts inspired, no doubt, in part by the annual changes from the melancholy long winter nights to the cheery midnight sun of summer. Others remind us of the green and smiling valleys referred to. The emotional range of Grieg's songs is, indeed, very great, as we shall see in analyzing them separately; and it must be remembered that we have here only fifty out of one hundred and thirty-five. Patriotism is a sentiment frequently embodied in them, and so is the allied *Heimweh*,—the longing for home of which our No. 33 is such an eloquent example. There is infinite tenderness in some of these *Lieder*, and while a few of the earliest ones (not included in this volume) are commonplace, none of them are tainted and diseased, like so much modern music. To cite a few sentences from my book on Grieg: "One of the most remarkable traits of Grieg is that although he had an invalid body nearly all his life, his artist soul was always healthy; there is not a trace of the morbid or mawkish in his music, but, on the contrary, a superb virility and an exuberant joyousness such as are supposed to be inseparable from robust health. The tenderness just referred to is not incompatible with this sturdy virility; tenderness

Norwegian wild songs into his flower-pots—was very widely prevalent. After reading this book he wrote to the author, under date of December 30, 1905: "Of particular importance is the chapter on the relation of Norwegian folk-songs to my originality. For this I am extremely grateful to you, for you have succeeded brilliantly in rehabilitating me in the face of the many unjust and ignorant foreign criticisms."

is a modern trait of the best manhood; Homer's heroes had none of it."

To sum up: the emotional range of Grieg's songs is wide, their subjects are poetic and pictorial, there are single pages in them that contain more of the essence of genius than many whole sonatas, symphonies, and operas. That some of the best of these songs are known to few may seem strange; but the mystery is explained by the fact that to do justice to such poetic products a vocalist must be not only technically expert, but a person of deep feeling and able to enter into the spirit of something so rich and strange as Grieg's "fjord music." How many vocalists of that sort are there? Some day there will be more, and then Grieg's songs will be second in vogue to none.

Ffrangcon Davies relates in his book, *The Singing of the Future*, that when he sought Sims Reeves's aid in regard to the singing of *Elijah* the first words of that eminent artist to his pupil were: "What do you think about the Prophet —what sort of man was he?"

There is a wealth of suggestion in that question, to singers of songs as well as of oratorios. "What sort of *poem* is this that I am about to sing?" is the first question vocalists should ask themselves. Wagner suggested that in studying one of his operas the first thing to do was for the singers to have a meeting and read their parts, as if it were simply a play. In the same way, a singer should first study the poem of a song, and fathom its inner spirit before taking up the music. If this were more frequently done there would be larger audiences at song recitals, and fewer unfortunates like General Grant, who, when a young lady asked his permission to sing a song for him, asked, "Is it long?"

The following brief notes are offered in the hope of helping amateurs as well as professionals to present the Grieg songs with a fuller understanding of their contents. The new translations made specially for this volume will also facilitate that task. Grieg himself was very critical regarding the translations of his songs into other languages, and with some of them he was greatly displeased, because the poetry had been impaired and the accents displaced.

A word of explanation is due regarding the texts used in this edition. The plan of *The Musicians Library* has been to print the songs in English and in the original language. If in this case German is used instead of Norwegian it is because there are in this country nine times as many Germans as Norwegians, and probably a proportionate number of singers and music lovers. The editor is glad to be able to assure the readers of these pages that Grieg would have approved the choice of his songs made for this volume, for he wrote to him, after reading *Songs and Song Writers*: "Always the critics have pointed out my least important things as the best, and unfortunately also *vice versâ*. How happy I am that this is not the case with you. You have in the main dwelt on the very songs which I myself consider the best."

1. *Morning Dew (Morgenthau)*. Written in 1863, the year after Grieg had passed his examination at the Leipzig Conservatory, this love-song harks back to Leipzig impressions. The poem is by a German, Chamisso, who was noted as a naturalist beside being one of the most popular writers of lyrics.

2. *My Mind is like a Peak Snow-crowned (Mein Sinn ist wie der mächt'ge Fels)*. This passionate and impetuous love-song was written in the same year as the preceding number and likewise betrays the influence of the German masters, notably Schubert, whose *Aufenthalt* it suggests. The poem is by Andersen, Denmark's most prolific and popular author, among whose thirty-three volumes are the *Fairy Tales* which have made his name a household word throughout the world.

3. *I Love Thee (Ich liebe Dich)*. Of all the one hundred and thirty-five songs of Grieg this one is the most popular. Though entirely original, it might have been, as stated on another page of this volume, written by Schumann in one of his most inspired moments. It is a musical love-letter, dated 1864, the year when Grieg became engaged to his cousin, Nina Hagerup. For

her it was written, and never has a composer poured out his feelings more intensely, more overwhelmingly, for the object of his adoration. The daughter of a famous Danish actress, she was ideally suited to being Grieg's wife. "She is short and somewhat broad," wrote Mrs. Finck, when we visited them at Troldhaugen in July, 1901, "with a face that her photographs do not do justice to, because there is a peculiar mixture of shyness and vivacity that eludes the camera; she has gray hair, cut short, and very intelligent, dark blue eyes." Tchaikovsky had written three years previously that she was "just as small, fragile, and sympathetic" as her husband; that he had never "met a better informed or more highly cultivated woman;" and that he found her "as amiable, as gentle, as childishly simple and without guile as her celebrated husband." She sang his songs, sometimes in public (the last time, before Queen Victoria in 1898), as no one else could sing them. Her art reminded Frau von Holstein of Jenny Lind's "in its captivating *abandon*, dramatic vivacity, soulful treatment of the poem, and unaffected manner." Grieg himself once wrote to the editor of this volume: "My best songs were composed for her; they embody my personal feelings, and I could no more have stopped expressing them in songs than I could have stopped breathing." It seemed to him "a matter of course that one should sing so beautifully, so eloquently, so soulfully, as she did."

4. *The Poet's Heart* (*Des Dichters Herz*). Another Andersen poem, set to music in the same year as *I Love Thee*. The expression mark *allegro molto ed agitato*—very fast and impassioned—indicates the keynote of this effusion of the poet, who maintains excitedly that however urgent may be the ocean-waves, however fragrant the flowers, wild the winds, they are as naught compared with the exuberant emotions in the poet's bleeding heart.

5. *Cradle Song* (*Wiegenlied*). Not a cradle song in the usual sense of the term is this ineffably sad effusion. It is a dirge sung by the father, for the mother who died in giving life to her boy;

and the father confesses he would have slain himself to join her had it not been for the child's need of a protector. In 1899, when the editor of this volume was writing his book on *Songs and Song Writers*, he asked Grieg for some details regarding his songs. After some hesitation, the composer kindly forwarded him a letter of thirty-six pages full of valuable information. In this letter he referred to the *Wiegenlied*. A few years previously he was dismayed to find it in the programme of a concert given at the Gewandhaus. It seemed to him impossible in a concert hall because of its very *intime* character. But —the vocalist was Johannes Messchaert, and Arthur Nikisch played the piano part. After a few lines had been sung, deep silence prevailed in the hall. The composer's hopes began to rise, because the performance was so incomparably beautiful. And when the last bar had been sung, the audience expressed its satisfaction in an outburst of prolonged applause. Note the expression mark, "not too slow, but very mournfully." The piano part is *pianissimo* throughout; the accents must be very subtle, yet distinct. The intense grief, combined with the lulling tenderness that belongs to a cradle song, gives this *Lied* a unique place in musical literature. The author of the poem, Andreas Munch, enjoys great popularity in Norway; the parliament granted him an honorary pension. His best work is his *Sorrow and Comfort*, in which he bewails the death of his wife.

6. *Autumn Storm* (*Herbststurm*). Concert singers with dramatic gifts will find this a most effective number. It is longer than most of Grieg's songs and presents excellent opportunities for climaxing. The text, by the eminent Danish poet, Christian Richardt (who is particularly noted for his pictures of nature in diverse aspects), imperatively called for such a setting. It presents a vivid suggestion of the advent of winter in the North, and Grieg's music is equally realistic, recalling both the stormy aspect of approaching winter and its domestic comforts and consolations.

7, 8. *Ragnhild; Ragna*. In 1866 Grieg and the

poet Drachmann made an excursion to the Norwegian mountains. One day they became acquainted with some charming women who at once inspired the poet and the composer to utter their sentiments in joint song. The result of this collaboration appeared as opus 44, entitled *From the Mountains and the Fjords*, with the subtitle *Souvenirs of a Trip in Norway*. It consists of a prologue, an epilogue, and between them the two buoyant songs *Ragnhild* and *Ragna*, which are as tuneful and almost as simple as folksongs, yet unmistakably Griegian. They speak for themselves.

9. *Margaret's Cradle Song (Margarethens Wiegenlied)*. Although the poem underlying this number is by the Norwegian Ibsen, the music seems like a reminiscence of the days Grieg spent as a youth amid the chorals and folk-songs of Germany and the songs of Franz. But when we reach bars 10-18 we realize our mistake: it is a Norwegian baby, after all, that Ibsen and Grieg are singing about. The song is both a lullaby and a prayer—how different from the heart-rending dirge of No. 5 in our collection!

10. *Woodland Wandering (Waldwanderung)*. Here is a song of love and summer—a merry woodland song that everybody can understand and enjoy at first hearing, including even those men who never go to anything but "musical comedies." The melody is so simple and trips along so lightly that one might fancy it had been invented by a shepherd boy instead of by the greatest master of subtle harmony since Wagner and Liszt.

11. *Mother Sorrow (Mutterschmerz)*. The poet who, in No. 6, took us to the heart of nature, here bares the heart of a poor mother who has lost her infant boy and prays for more tears to weep. It is a most tender, pathetic song. A grief like this came into the life of Grieg and his wife. In the words of his intimate friend, Frank Van der Stucken: "Grieg liked children very much, and used to speak about a child of his, a girl, that had died very young. How tenderly he would

mention her name and relate incidents of her short life!" It was Mr. Van der Stucken who added a second German verse to Grieg's song *I Love Thee* for the Peters edition.

12. *Good Morning (Guten Morgen)*. This song is a good illustration of how much the combined imaginative powers of a poet and a composer can make of the simple idea of daybreak. It is one of Grieg's most joyous songs.

13. *First Meeting (Erstes Begegnen)*. Another Björnson song, on the dawn of love. This eminent poet has played almost as important a part in the political life of Norway as in its literature. He and Grieg were for several decades intimate friends; they collaborated not only in a number of songs but also in larger works, like *Olaf Trygvason* (an operatic fragment), the men's chorus *Landsighting*, and the melodious and pathetic *At the Cloister Gate*, which cannot be too highly commended to music clubs commanding a women's choir and a soprano and an alto soloist.

14. *From Monte Pincio (Vom Monte Pincio)*. The Pincio, in Rome, used to be known as the "hill of gardens." Here two thousand years ago were the famous gardens of the millionaire Lucullus, and many memories of mediaeval events are associated with the place, too. At present it is a fashionable resort and drive, and in the evening, when there is music, it presents a gay scene. Björnson touches on the various points of view which occur to a poet's observant and reminiscent mind on a visit to this picturesque place; and Grieg's music, with a realistic art worthy of both Schubert and Liszt, reproduces all these aspects in his music—the glowing sunset, the swarming people, the domes of the city below, the mists calling up dim memories of the past and prophecies as to a future awakening of Rome to her former glory. Note how the opening chords conjure up the sunset mood; how the music grows funereal at the words "face of the dead;" note the echo-like sounds of the mountain horns; the fine contrast provided by the recurring gay melody (*vivo*); and many other exquisite details.

15. *The Princess* (*Die Prinzessin*). Another immortal mastersong—Griegish in every bar of the melody and harmony, as individual, as original almost as if no one had written songs before Grieg. Sing it, play it, twice, twenty times, two hundred times, you will like it more and more, and it will haunt you like the face of a beautiful girl illumined by love. How exquisitely Björnson's Heine-like story of the princess in her castle overcome by the lay of the minstrel below, is mirrored in the music! How grandly the chords near the close sink with the setting sun!

16. *My Song to the Spring I proffer* (*Dem Lenz soll mein Lied erklingen*). With *Monte Pincio* and *The Princess* we entered the second phase of Grieg's activity, in which his individuality manifests itself strongly, and Norwegian local color becomes more and more vivid. No. 16 also is thoroughly characteristic of its composer. To enter fully into the spirit of this greeting to spring, the singer should bear in mind that if the coming of spring is a joyous event to us who live in temperate latitudes, it is doubly so to the Norseman, who not only has missed the murmuring of the brooks and the blooming of the flowers, but has not even seen the light of the sun, for months. Spring to him is like the release from a dark dungeon, and it begets that "unbounded joy and cheerfulness" which we have noted as a Norwegian characteristic.

17. *At a Young Woman's Bier* (*An der Bahre einer jungen Frau*). There is a world of sorrow in the spectacle of a man standing at the bier of his wife, cut off in her youth—a world of sorrow which finds its most poignant expression in this deep-felt song. It is pathetic, tragic, to the end; but conspicuous for thrilling, tear-compelling beauty are the nine bars from the twelfth to the twentieth, which are like a vision of heaven granted to the mourner. Had Grieg written nothing but those nine bars he would still be one of the immortal masters.

18. *Hidden Love* (*Verborg'ne Liebe*). The story

of a maiden and a youth who love one another while neither ever discovers the secret is a favorite one with the poets. Björnson's poem might have been written in any country, but Grieg's setting of it is music such as the world never heard before he began to compose. It is Norse music, and the expert ear also detects melodic steps which illustrate the strange relationship between Scandinavian and Oriental art.

19. *Solvejg's Song* (*Solvejgs Lied*). Grieg once wrote to the editor of this volume that *Solvejg's Song* was the only one of his songs which contains a borrowed melody. The allegretto section, in particular, has the lilt of a folk-song; but the harmonies are, of course, his own. None of Grieg's songs is sung oftener than this; even Patti added it to her repertory a few years ago. Solvejg (pronounced Solevīg) is the heroine of *Peer Gynt*, Ibsen's famous drama. She falls in love with Peer Gynt notwithstanding his rough peasant ways. But he has fantastic aspirations to become emperor of the world, and soon leaves her to seek adventures in diverse countries, including Arabia. She remains in the hut he had built for her in the Norwegian forest, and her song attests that her thoughts and her heart are with him always.

20. *Solvejg's Slumber Song* (*Solvejgs Wiegenlied*). No more than No. 5 in our collection is this a cradle song in the usual sense of the word. It is the ineffably sad dirge which Solvejg sings when Peer Gynt has at last returned to her, only to die in her arms. No singer, unless she is an artist of the highest rank or has suffered the same grief in her life, can fathom the depth of the sorrow here expressed in tones of exquisite tenderness. The creative thrill of delight which Grieg must have felt when he penned this song—especially the last twelve bars, which have not their equal in more than a dozen other songs ever composed—must have atoned for all the sufferings of his life. As the editor has said elsewhere: "This death song closes the quasi-operatic score of *Peer Gynt*, and if there is, excepting *Tristan and Isolde*, an opera which has a more

deeply emotional or a more sorrowful ending, I have not heard it."

21. *A Swan* (*Ein Schwan*). This is not only one of the most popular songs in modern concert halls, but is also one of the grandest ever composed. No one should attempt to sing it unless endowed with sufficient dramatic feeling to bring out the deeper meaning of Ibsen's poem, the varied expression, and, especially, the superb climax where the swan, after a lifelong silence, sings at last. Grieg, in a letter to the editor, wished him to call particular attention to the fact that the words "Ja, da, da sangst du" should be sung "*sempre fortissimo*, if possible even with a *crescendo*, and by no means *diminuendo* and *piano*."

22. *The First Primrose* (*Mit einer Primula Veris*). Perhaps this is the best of all the Grieg songs for a first introduction to his style. Its ravishing melody enraptures the senses at a first hearing, and every one will agree that it is the loveliest of spring songs. All the delicacy of a flower, the fragrance of May, the buoyancy of youth, are in this song of a lover who offers the first primrose of the season to his beloved in exchange for her heart. " When I first heard it, I was affected as I was when I saw my first Mariposa Lily in California."

23. *With a Water-Lily* (*Mit einer Wasserlilie*). Ibsen's poems always inspired Grieg to his best efforts. One day when Madame Grieg had sung her husband's setting of Ibsen's songs for him, he shook hands with both and whispered one word, "Understood!" In the *Water-lily* song, as in the others, Grieg has musically "understood" his great countryman. It is aptly named an *allegro grazioso*, the melody poising on the chords as the lilies on their slender stems. The variety amid the unity of the accompaniment suggests the skill with which Schubert voices the brook in his songs of the Miller's Maid.

24. *Minstrel's Song* (*Spielmannslied*). Another gem of the first water, Grieg in every bar, thoroughly Ibsenish and Norwegian. The poem embodies the favorite Norse legend of the river sprite teaching the magic love-compelling art of song in exchange for the singer's salvation. In this case the lover loses his beloved as well as his soul. The music starts in the manner of a legend and develops into a miniature drama. It is a song which afterwards haunted the composer himself; following the example of Schubert, he made it the theme of a piece of chamber music—his splendid string quartet, of which it colors three movements, and which, as he informed the editor of this volume, was written in the country after his soul had been harrowed by heartrending experiences.

25. *'T was on a Lovely Eve in June* (*Am schönsten Sommerabend war's*). In this poem by J. Paulsen, one of Norway's favorite bards, we behold a Norse maiden tending her goats, knitting and gazing dreamily over the fjord. The music is an exact echo of the poem, engendering the same summery mood. Heed the *dolce e tranquillo!* The last bars have a peculiarly haunting quality, and they illustrate one of the most captivating of Grieg's musical traits,—his utter avoidance of the commonplace, particularly at the end of a song or piece, where so many composers are careless, forgetting that all's well that ends well.

26. *The Youth* (*Der Bursch*). The high-water mark of Grieg's genius is represented by the nine songs from Nos. 26 to 34 in this collection. They belong in a group of twelve, concerning which Grieg wrote to the editor in 1900: "I was all aflame with enthusiasm when I became acquainted in the spring of 1880 with the poems of Vinje, which embody a deep philosophy of life; and in the course of eight to ten days I composed not only the songs contained in the fourth volume, but others by the same poet which are not yet in print. A. O. Vinje was a peasant by birth. He attempted with his prose works to enlighten the Norwegian people, and these writings, together with his poems, gave him a great national importance." *Der Bursch* is one of those songs which indicate that despair in the Far North, with its sunless winters, must be a more

hopeless feeling than elsewhere. And the music! How weird its melodic intervals, how disconsolate its strange harmonies! Here we breathe the very air of Norway; there is a tone of Norwegian *Volkstümlichkeit*, which was new at that time,—new in music, new in Grieg, as he himself has said.

27. *Springtide* (*Der Frühling*). When Tchaikovsky heard Nina Grieg sing this heavenly song in Leipzig he was moved to tears; and he showed his gratitude subsequently for the great pleasure given, by sending her his own songs, with a cordial dedication. What melodic breadth, what exquisite tenderness, what superbly swelling harmonies and entrancing modulations from key to key, are in this *Lied!*

28. *The Wounded Heart* (*Der Verwundete*). This exquisitely Griegish song is closely associated with the foregoing, not only as following it in the same series, but because the composer arranged them for string orchestra, in which version they were published under the title of *Two Elegiac Melodies*. They are often heard in concert halls. In a letter to the editor, Grieg explained that while in the songs themselves the profound melancholy of the poems explains the sombre strains of the music, the orchestral version, having no explanatory verses, called for more significant titles, wherefore he called them *The Last Spring* and *Heart-Wounds*.

29. *At the Brookside* (*An einem Bache*). This is one of the best songs for studying—and enjoying—the peculiar melodic intervals and harmonies of Grieg. Every bar seems to have the five letters of his name stamped on it, and the charm of this original musical physiognomy grows on you like the expression of a face that indicates character as well as beauty. There are here melodic steps and harmonic progressions so strange that the uninitiated may almost suspect them to be misprints; but gradually, as the ear becomes habituated to them, they assume an unearthly beauty.

30. *A Vision* (*Was ich sah*). A song depicting the effect of love at first sight—love which failed of fruition and now lives on remembrance only.

31. *The Old Mother* (*Die alte Mutter*). A charming song of filial love and gratitude which shows that the romantic infatuation for a beautiful girl is not the only kind of emotion that inspires immortal tone-poems. Here the music is not so inseparably associated with the poem as in *Monte Pincio* or *A Swan*; but what a glorious melody, what quaint original harmonies! Original harmonies the composers of our time can still write; but who will pen a melody like this?

32. *The Only Thing* (*Das Erste*). This song might be considered a commentary on Otway's lines:

"O woman! lovely woman! Nature made thee
To temper man: we had been brutes without you."

33. *On the Journey Home* (*Auf der Reise zur Heimath*). Vinje's poem gives expression to the emotions of one who has been away from home and returns to see again the familiar fertile valleys, the snow mountains, and to hear his mother-tongue once more. It struck a deeply responsive chord in Grieg's heart, which always remained in Norway when he resided for the time elsewhere,—patriotism and love of home being two of the strongest traits in his character. This whole song is of indescribable beauty. Attention is called particularly to the last four bars, in which the composer is overwhelmed with emotion as the memories of youth come back to him. These final bars are a fervent and glorious outburst of feeling, for which few parallels exist in the whole range of music. Note, further, the refreshingly unconventional and poetic ending.

34. *Friendship* (*Ein Freundschaftsstück*). The title of this song is obviously sarcastic, as the first four words indicate. All friends are false, the poet wails, because one has stolen away another's chosen spouse. Poignant grief has never been expressed more bitterly than in Grieg's setting of these lines. The strange, weird chords give the effect of an intensified minor. Among Grieg's songs this one occupies the same place that the gruesome *Doppelgänger* does among Schubert's.

35. *Greeting (Gruss)*. Grieg had a habit of keeping some of his songs in his desk for years before he considered them ripe for the public. When he died, a considerable number, written in the years 1865-1905, were found among his manuscripts, and these are to be issued by Peters in Leipzig. The year of publication does not always coincide with that of composition, and that is the reason why some of those in our collection are undated. As regards opus 48, to which *Gruss* and the following five numbers belong, the fact that all of them are settings of German poems might arouse the suspicion that they are early songs, written while Grieg was still betraying German influences; but a glance at any page (especially in the first two) will show this guess to be wide of the mark, for these songs reveal Grieg in all the maturity and individuality of his genius. The first of them, *Gruss*, is a setting of one of Heine's most famous poems.

36. *Ere Long, O Heart of Mine (Dereinst, Gedanke mein)*. "The realm of harmony was always my dream-world"—these words of Grieg are vividly recalled by his wonderful setting of Geibel's poem offering the peace of the grave as a solace for life's disappointments. Musicians sometimes hear in their dreams harmonies which seem more delicious, more thrilling, than any ever heard by them when awake. This song contains such dream-world harmonies, especially in bars 10-17, which are like a vision of peace and bliss beyond the grave. Excepting Liszt's setting of Goethe's *Ueber allen Gipfeln ist Ruh (O'er the Tree-tops all is at Rest)*, known as *Wanderer's Night Song* (included in *Fifty Mastersongs*), there is perhaps in the whole realm of music no song so ethereal as this. But let no one try to sing or play it who ignores the least expression mark, who knows not the difference between *pp* and *ppp*, or who cannot subtly accent and increase or decrease a tone even when singing or playing *ppp*.

37. *The Way of the World (Lauf der Welt)*. There are cases of infatuation where everything is understood without a formal proposal, and a kiss is granted as spontaneously as the first glance of love. Uhland's poem tells of such a case, and Grieg has added a merry musical commentary as spontaneous as the glance and the kiss. Here, as in most of the Grieg songs, much of the effect depends on the artistic use of the sustaining pedal. This song will some day have a sensational success in concert halls. The singers have not discovered it yet.

38. *The Silent Nightingale (Die verschwiegene Nachtigall)*. Walther von der Vogelweide was born about the year 1160, and he was the best lyric poet of mediaeval Germany, an inspired singer of *Minnelieder*, or songs of love. Grieg's music is as full of bird twitterings and flowers and trees as the poem. Bars 19-22 are particularly Griegish.

39. *In Time of Roses (Zur Rosenzeit)*. This is the only Goethe song in our collection. Germany's greatest poet was not free from jealousy, and there is reason to believe that he disapproved of some of Schubert's settings of his songs, not because he did not think them good enough, but because he thought them too good; the beauty of the music was likely to eclipse the poems! He might have felt the same way about Grieg's music to his *Rosenzeit*; yet such jealousy is foolish, for did not Schubert and Grieg simply translate the poems into music, retaining all their subtle charms and their moods?

40. *A Dream (Ein Traum)*. To Friedrich von Bodenstedt, better known as Mirza-Schaffy, Germany owes some of her choicest lyric poems. *Ein Traum* is a love-song in the Heine vein; Grieg has made of it a *Lied* which is perhaps the most effective of all his songs for the concert hall, rising at the end to a stirring climax.

41. *The Mother Sings (Die Mutter singt)*. When Grieg wrote this lugubrious heartrending song of the infant on the bier he was inspired by the mournful memories of his own daughter, who had died so young, and concerning whom Van der Stucken wrote: "How tenderly he would mention her name and relate incidents of her

short life!" Yet even the pain of a father's wounded heart does not fully explain the quiet but intensely agonizing spirit of this music. There is in it also that national sombreness which makes even some of the dances of the Norwegians seem more like the dirges of other nations, and which in the case of an actual dirge like this becomes simply heartrending. It is significant that this song is dedicated to Johannes Messchaert (see the comments on No. 5).

42. *In the Boat* (*Im Kahne*). Lilli Lehmann, Nordica, and Gadski often sing this song in the concert hall with splendid effect. It is a true song of the fjord, with glimpses of the water, the fishing, the dancing and love-making natives, the cries of the gulls. In No. 4 of this same opus, *A Bird cried o'er the Lonely Sea*, Grieg, as he informed the editor, embodied in the introductory bars a melodico-rhythmic motive which he heard from a gull in the Sognefjord; but as the music is on the whole less interesting, preference is here given to this other song of the fjord. It illustrates, among other things, the charm of Grieg's unexpected modulations, in which he equals Schubert.

43. *The Mountain Maid* (*Das Kind der Berge*). Grieg suffered a great deal from ill health, especially in the later years of his life; it left him little energy for composing, and that is why he wrote comparatively little during the last two years of his life. Yet what he did write was often equal to the best of what he composed in his more vigorous years. "But oh! the nights!" he wrote to Oscar Meyer in 1897. "Not to be able to get a wink of sleep, and to be almost choked with phlegm! Life is truly delightful!" he adds sarcastically. The following year he sent this friend proof-sheets of his new songs, opus 67 (subsequently published under the title of *The Mountain Maid*), concerning which he added this interesting information: "Kindly inform X [the English translator] that the subject concerns a peasant girl, and that the original therefore presents a national or folk-lore style. What a pity that you cannot read, in the original,

Garborg's lovely pastoral, *Hugtussa*, from which these poems have been taken! It is a masterpiece, full of simplicity and depth, and indescribably beautiful in color. That these songs (opus 67) are essentially different from any of my former ones cannot escape your fine perception of such things." Of the eight songs in opus 67, five deserve a place in our collection, but two of them (*Zickeltanz*—another favorite of Lilli Lehmann—and *Ein böser Tag*) must reluctantly be omitted. No. 2, *The Mountain Maid*, is one of the very best of the Grieg songs, delightfully melodious, harmonically quaint and original. It combines the freshness of youth with the depth of mature genius, and a touch of the Norwegian melancholy.

44. *The Tryst* (*Stelldichein*). A love-song with the warm blood of youth in its veins. Note the energetic pulse of the middle voices in the pianoforte part. Destined to become a favorite.

45. *Love* (*Liebe*). Another ardent love-song, with the hall-mark of Grieg stamped on every bar. An unquenchable fire, like that of *Tristan*, warms this music. If all the world loves a lover, all the world cannot fail to love this love-song.

46. *At Mother's Grave* (*Am Grabe der Mutter*). In 1900 Grieg wrote to the editor of this volume that he had ready for the autumn a further collection of songs which would be "of a cosmopolitan character." They show, as some of the songs of his second period do, that he had learned from Wagner (as he frankly admitted) to perfect his declamation. We have room for only two of them. In *At Mother's Grave* we find the composer once more in his most mournful mood. This *Lento Funebre* is really a funeral march, most poignant in its expression of grief. It would undoubtedly make an impressive orchestral dirge. The editor once wrote to Grieg suggesting he should make an orchestral funeral march of this song, but tore up the letter for fear Grieg might see something ominous in such a suggestion, at his age, and with his very poor health.

47. *Dreams* (*Träume*). This story of a lover who, failing to win the object of his fancy, finds consolation in dreaming of her, but loses even that pleasure on awaking, is not taken by the composer too seriously. There are plenty of fish in the sea! But it is good music, cosmopolitan, and with no suggestion of the fjord.

48. *Eros.* Concert singers will find this a valuable number for their purposes. There is less of the essence of Grieg in it than in most of these songs, but it has "go," and at the end there is an imposing climax.

49, 50. *Radiant Night* (*Lichte Nacht*); *Take Good Heed* (*Sieh' dich vor*). While Number 49 is sufficiently cosmopolitan to please even that German critic who objected to Grieg because he "stuck in the fjord," No. 50 takes us back to the fjord, where most of us like him best,—the fjord, where he sang his loveliest melodies and dreamed his quaintest harmonies. As Leonard Liebling has aptly remarked: "It is stupid to reproach Grieg with being too national. Had he been less so he would not now be universal. That is a curious paradox in music. See Tchaikovsky, Dvořák, Smetana, Verdi, Wagner, and others,"—notably Chopin.

Henry T. Finck

New York, September 15, 1908.

Fifty Songs
for High Voice

MORNING DEW
(MORGENTHAU)

(Composed in 1868)

(Original Key, A)

ADELBERT von CHAMISSO (1781-1838)
English version by Nathan Haskell Dole

EDVARD GRIEG, Op. 4, Nº 2

The Sun is the sor - row - bring - er, The Night scat - ters tears as she
Die Son - ne, die bringt viel Lei - den, es wei - net die schei - den - de

flies; I al - so must weep and not lin - ger— The
Nacht; ich al - so muss wei - nen und schei - den, es.

world now has o - pen'd its eyes,___ its___ eyes.___
ist ja die Welt schon er - wacht,___ schon er - wacht.___

MY MIND IS LIKE A PEAK SNOW-CROWNED
(MEIN SINN IST WIE DER MÄCHT'GE FELS)

HANS CHRISTIAN ANDERSEN (1805 – 1875)
English version by Nathan Haskell Dole
German version by F. von Holstein

(Composed in 1868)

(Original Key, *C minor*)

EDVARD GRIEG, Op.5, №4

Allegro molto agitato

VOICE

PIANO

fp *cresc.* *con Pedale* *f*

My / Mein

mind is like a peak snow - crown'd
Sinn ist wie der mächt - 'ge Fels,

f

That tow'rs a - loft to the
der hoch zum Him - - - mel sich

skies;
thürmt;

p

My heart is like the
Mein Herz ist wie das

p

self in my heart thou dwell - est, Where might - y storm bil - lows
selbst a - ber lebst im Her - zen, da to - sen Bran - dun - gen

surge, Where might - y storm bil - lows surge, Where
wild, da to - sen Bran - dun - gen wild, da

might - y storm bil - lows surge. _____
to - sen Bran - dun - gen wild! _____

I LOVE THEE
(ICH LIEBE DICH)

(Composed in 1864)

(Original Key)

HANS CHRISTIAN ANDERSEN (1805-1875)
English version by Auber Forestier
German version by F von Holstein

EDVARD GRIEG, Op. 5, № 3

THE POET'S HEART
(DES DICHTERS HERZ)

(Composed in 1864)

(Original Key)

HANS CHRISTIAN ANDERSEN (1805-1875)
English version by Nathan Haskell Dole
German version by F. von Holstein

EDVARD GRIEG, Op. 5, № 2

The in-fi-nite course of the waves who can tell? You know not the soul that in mu-sic doth dwell;
Be - greifst du des Mee - res Wo - gen-drang? den Geist der Tö - ne im Sai - ten-klang?

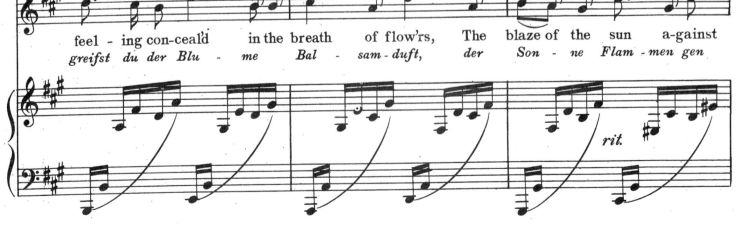

feel-ing con-ceal'd in the breath of flow'rs, The blaze of the sun a-gainst
greifst du der Blu - me Bal - sam-duft, der Son - ne Flam-men gen

11

CRADLE SONG
(WIEGENLIED)

(Composed in 1865)

(Original Key, G♯ minor)

A. MUNCH (1811-1884)
English version by Nathan Haskell Dole
German version by Edmund Lobedanz

EDVARD GRIEG, Op. 9, № 2

Non lento, ma molto doloroso

VOICE

p

1. Sleep, my son, oh, slum - ber well!
2. Sleep, my son, sleep pla - cid - ly!
3. Nev - er thy sweet morn - ing-joy
4. Dost thou feel thy moth - er dear

1. *Schlaf,' mein Sohn, und schlumm' - re suss,*
2. *Schlaf,' mein Herz - chen, traüm' von ihr,*
3. *Nie soll sei - ne schwe - re Brust*
4. *Ob wohl dei - ne Müt - ter sich*

PIANO

pp

Ped.   ❀ Ped.   ❀ Ped.

Cra - dle works the sooth - ing spell;   Ay, al - tho'____ the
Here thy fa - ther sits by thee,   Rocks thee with____ un -
Shall his cru - el grief de - stroy;   Nev - er shall____ thy
O'er thine in - no - cence hov - 'ring near?   Dost thou see____ her

Wieg - lein ist dein Pa - ra - dies.   Ach, die dir____ das
Va - ter sit - zet hier bei dir,   wie - get dich____ mit
trü - ben dei - ne Mor - gen - lust,   nie - mals soll____ dein
neigt im Schlum - mer ü - ber dich?   Lachst ja oft____ so

Ped.   ❀ Ped.   ❀ Ped.   ❀

grave so cold   Doth thy gen - tle moth - er
prac - tised skill,   Would pro - tect thee from _____ all
mer - ry eyes   Bit - ter tears in his _____ sur -
in thy dreams   When thy smile in an - swer

Le - ben gab,   lie - get in dem kal - ten
treu - em Muth,   schir - met dich mit Leib und
Kin - des-Glück   schau - en sei - ner Thrä - nen
süss und rein,   siehst du dann dein Müt - ter

Ped.   ❀   Ped.   ❀   Ped.   ❀

5. Sleep, my son, oh, slum - ber well, Cra - dle works the
5. *Schlaf,* *mein Sohn,* *und schlumm' - re süss,* *Wieg - lein ist dein*

sooth - ing spell; Ay al - tho'___ the grave so cold
Pa - ra - dies, *ach,* *die dir___ das Le - ben gab,*

Doth thy gen - tle moth - - er hold.
lie - get in dein kal - - ten Grab.

AUTUMN STORM
(HERBSTSTURM)

(Composed in 1865)

C. RICHARDT (1831-1892)
English version by Nathan Haskell Dole
German version by F. von Holstein

(*Original Key, D*)

EDVARD GRIEG, Op.18, № 4

sum - mer the for - est was green, so green, And mer - ry birds sang from
Som - mer wie war da so grün der Wald, als Zwit - schern von je - dem

ff con fuoco

morn till e'en. Then blew the tem-pest his pow-er-ful horn; The
Zweig er-schallt: Da blies der Sturm sein ge - wal - ti - ges Lied, und

clus - ter-ing leaves with af - fright were torn; A - gain did he blow— his
Zit - tern und Ban - gen den Wald durch-zieht! Zum zwei - ten Mal blies er mit

horn with might: Then fad- ed the for - est's crown so bright. When
neu - er Wuth, da bleich-te des Wal - des grü - ne Gluth. Beim

thrice he had blown, the leaves on the gale All flut - ter'd a - way mid sleet and hail.
drit - ten Mal sank ein je - des Laub, es flat - tern die Blät - ter in den Staub.

Poco Andante

But need-y folk prize the spoil of storm:
Die Ar-men nur freut des Sturms Gesaus':

They gath-er them fag-gots to keep them warm;
sie sam-meln sich Brennholz für's en-ge Haus;

And Win-ter, al-beit he's
doch ist auch der Win-ter

hard as steel, The wounds that he made him-self will heal! He
hart ge-nug, er hei-let die Wun-de, die selbst er schlug. Er

Più vivo

spreads out his man-tle soft and white,
hüllt in den Man-tel, weiss und weich,

On ev-'ry place where the
wohl je-de Wun-de in

RAGNHILD

(Composed in 1866)

(*Original Key*)

HOLGER DRACHMANN (1846-   )*
English version by Charles Fonteyn Manney
German version by Wilhelm Henzen

EDVARD GRIEG, Op.44, № 3

When I saw you, dear one,
Ach! als ich, du Trau - te,

Light-ly come on board,   New and ten-der mean-ing   Fill'd the sounds I heard;
dich ge-seh'n an Bord: Al - les, was ich schau-te,   sprach ein neu - es Wort;

Land and sea were   ring-ing   With   a won-drous sing-ing;
Fjord und Fel-sen   klan-gen,   schier als ob sie san-gen,

*d. 1908

As— we sail'd a - long,— We too
wie— das Boot hin - glitt,— san - gen

sang their song.—
selbst wir mit.—

When our voyage was o - ver End - ed was the spell,
Als die Fahrt ge - en - det, hör' es ach! noch jetzt—

And thy sweet lips fal - ter'd In a last fare - well.
wur - de mir ge - spen - det ihr Leb-wohl zu - letzt.

Where the moun - tains tow - er,
wo sich Fel - sen reck - ten,

Where the mead - ows
wo sich Glet - scher

flow - er,
streck - ten,

O - ver vio - let snows____
in____ der All - na - tur____

Ragn - hild's im - age glows!____
sah____ ich Ragn - hild nur!____

RAGNA

(Composed in 1866)

(*Original Key*)

HOLGER DRACHMANN (1846-)*
English version by Charles Fonteyn Manney
German version by Wilhelm Henzen

EDVARD GRIEG, Op.44, № 5

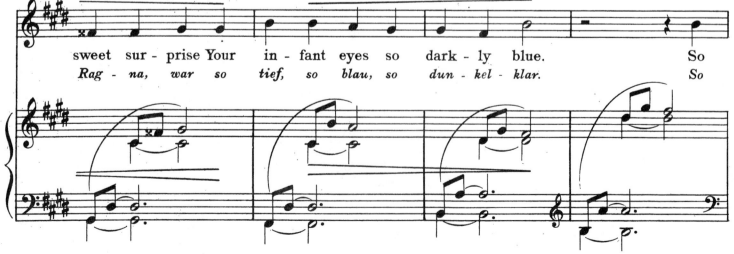

*d. 1908

MARGARET'S CRADLE SONG
(MARGARETHENS WIEGENLIED)

(Composed in 1868)

(Original Key)

HENRIK IBSEN (1828-1906)
English version by Arthur Westbrook
German version by F. von Holstein

EDVARD GRIEG, Op. 15, № 1

WOODLAND WANDERING
(WALDWANDERUNG)

HANS CHRISTIAN ANDERSEN (1805-1875)
English version by Arthur Westbrook
German version by F. von Holstein

(Composed in 1869)

(Original Key)

EDVARD GRIEG, Op. 18, № 1

MOTHER SORROW
(MUTTERSCHMERZ)

(Composed in 1870)

(Original Key)

C. RICHARDT (1831-1892)
English version by Nathan Haskell Dole
German version by F. von Holstein

EDVARD GRIEG, Op. 15, №4

1. Did you see my
2. Ten - der Je - sus,

1. Sahst du wohl mein
2. Mil - der Je - sus,

lit - tle lad, with his hair so curl - y and bright?_____
it was hard, when you took him back un - to you._____
Knäb - lein klein mit den Aug' so hell und so klug?_____
du warst hart, der du ihn zu den Ster - nen ent - ruckt._____

All day long I gazed at him, and ev - er with de - light.
Must you have an - oth - er an - gel, when earth has so few!
Sah ihn oft so lan - ge an und sah doch nie ge - nus.
Brauch - test du ein En - ge - lein? Du nahmst, was mich be - glückt.

Ah! how emp - ty, ah! how emp - ty now his cra - dle's ly - ing!
Did you give him shin - ing wings and heav - en's ra - diance glow - ing?
Ach, wie leer, wie leer, wie leer steht sei - ne Wieg' am Mor - gen,
Gabst du ihm ein Flü - gel - paar? Lässt Him - mels - freud' ihm schei - nen?

While my wretch-ed heart is full of deep de-spair and sigh - ing.
Oh, help me, so sore be-reft, and set my tears to flow - ing.
a - ber ach, die Brust wie voll von Seh - nen, Leid und Sor - gen.
Hilf mir, die ich freu-den-bar, o hilf, dass ich kann wei - nen.

molto legato

pp

rit.

a tempo

molto rit.

pp

GOOD MORNING!
(GUTEN MORGEN!)

(Composed in 1870)

(Original Key)

BJÖRNSTERNE BJÖRNSON (1832-)*
English version by Nathan Haskell Dole
German version by F. von Holstein

EDVARD GRIEG, Op. 21, № 2

*d. 1910

FIRST MEETING
(ERSTES BEGEGNEN)

(Composed in 1870)

(*Original Key*)

BJÖRNSTERNE BJÖRNSON (1832-   )*
English version by Nathan Haskell Dole
German version by F. von Holstein

EDVARD GRIEG, Op. 21, № 1

*d. 1910

FROM MONTE PINCIO
(VOM MONTE PINCIO)

NOCTURNE
(Composed in 1870)

(Original Key)

BJÖRNSTJERNE BJÖRNSON (1882 -   ) *
English version by F. Corder
German version by W. Henzen

EDVARD GRIEG, Op. 39, № 1

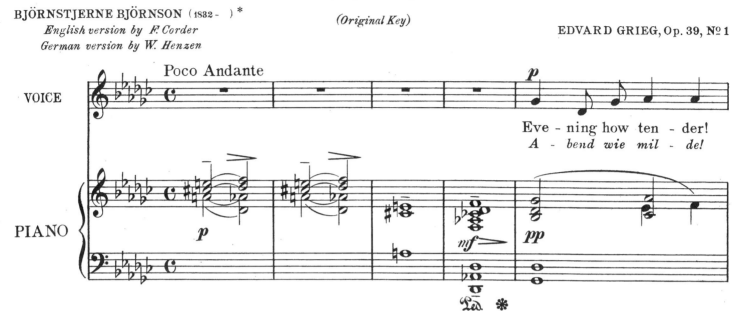

Eve - ning how ten - der!
A - bend wie mil - de!

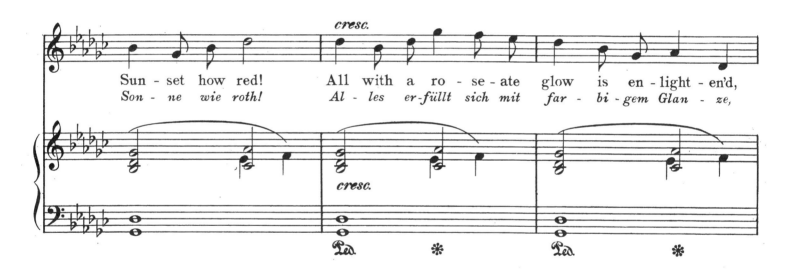

Sun - set how red! All with a ro - se - ate glow is en - light - en'd,
Son - ne wie roth! Al - les er - füllt sich mit far - bi - gem Glan - ze,

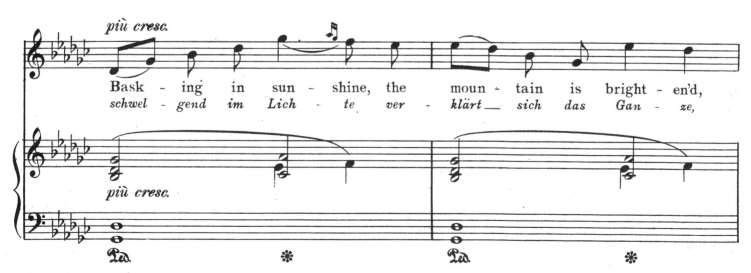

Bask - ing in sun - shine, the moun - tain is bright - en'd,
schwel - gend im Lich - te ver - klärt___ sich das Gan - ze,

*d. 1910

Vivo

Gleam-eth all red and warm, Eve-ning falls, peo - ple swarm; Moun - tain horns
Al - les glüht roth und warm, A - bend-schein, Vol - kes-schwarm; Al - les glüht:

p leggiero

poco rall.

sound a-bove, Flow - er - scent, looks of love.
Horn - mu - sik, Blu - men - duft, hei - sser Blick

poco rall.

pp

Sempre vivo

un poco rit.

All heart could wish gleams and sounds sweet - ly near us, Yearn - ing for
Al - les be - gehrt, rings um - strahlt und um - tö - net, sehn - lich nach

un poco rit.

Presto

beau - ty to cheer us.
dem, was ver - söh - net.

p leggiero

Gleam - eth all red and warm.
Al - les glüht roth und warm.

Eve - ning falls,
A - bend - schein,

peo - ple swarm;
Vol - kes - schwarm;

Moun - tain horns
Al - les glüht:

sound a - bove,
Horn - mu - sik,

Flow - er scent,
Blu - men - duft,

looks of love.
hei - sser Blick.

But, like a bea - con, will Rome one day wa - ken, Bright - en the dark - ness of
Doch, ei - ne Leuch - te, wird Ro - ma er - star - ken, hel - len die Nacht von I -

It - a - ly for - sa - ken; Toc - sins will ech - o and
ta - li - ens Mar - ken; Glo - cken - ge - läu - te, Ka -

can - non will roar! Fierce - ly will blaze out the spir - it of yore.
no - nen - ge - dröhn! Flammend wird wie - der die Vor - zeit er - steh'n.

Wed-ding strain, sound a-main!   Flute so gay,   zith-er play!
Tö - ne denn, Hoch-zeit-sang.   *Zi - ther-spiel, Flö - ten-klang!*

Wed-ding strain,   sound a-main!   Flute so gay,
Tö - ne denn,   *Hoch - zeit - sang.*   *Zi - ther-spiel,*

zith- er play!
Flö - ten - klang!

THE PRINCESS
(DIE PRINZESSIN)
(Composed in 1871)

(Original Key)

BJÖRNSTERNE BJÖRNSON (1832-   ) *
English version by Nathan Haskell Dole
German version by F. von Holstein

EDVARD GRIEG, Op. 21, № 4

*d. 1910

up in her bow'r sat the Prin-cess-maid; The youth heard her words and no
sass die Prin-zes-sin im Frau-en-ge-mach. Es schwei-get der Kna-be, es

long-er he play'd. "Oh, why art thou si-lent, My
schweigt die Schal-mei. „Blas' wei-ter, o Klei-ner, er-

lad, prith-ee play, It car-ries my thoughts that would fly far a-way, As the
fül-le mir, ach! all' mei-ne Ge-dan-ken, einst schweif-ten sie frei, wenn die

sun goes down, As the sun goes down." High
Son-ne sank, wenn die Son-ne sank." Es

up in her bow'r sat the Prin - cess - maid; The youth took his horn and a -
sass die Prin - zes - sin im Frau - en - ge - mach; auf's Neu - e im Tha - le er -

gain sweet-ly play'd. Then wept she and sobb'd as the
tont die Schal - mei. Da weint sie hin - aus in den

day came to end: "O tell me, my God, what my feel - ings por - tend!" Then the
sin - ken - den Tag: „Wie weh mir im Her - zen, steh', Herr - gott, mir bei!" Und die

sun went down, Then the sun went down.
Son - ne sank, und die Son - ne sank.

MY SONG TO THE SPRING I PROFFER
(DEM LENZ SOLL MEIN LIED ERKLINGEN)

(Composed in 1872)

(Original Key)

BJÖRNSTERNE BJÖRNSON (1832-)*
English version by Nathan Haskell Dole
German version by F. von Holstein

EDVARD GRIEG, Op. 21, № 3

My song to the Spring I
Dem Lenz soll mein Lied er-

prof-fer, Tho' yet there is no＿ sign of her, My song to the Spring I
klin-gen, das helf' ihn zu-rück uns brin-gen. Dem Lenz soll mein Lied er-

prof-fer, For in-fi-nite yearn-ings wake, The twain now a com-pact make:
klin-gen, von Sehn-sucht so ü-ber-reich, die Bei-den ver-steh'n sich gleich.

*d. 1910

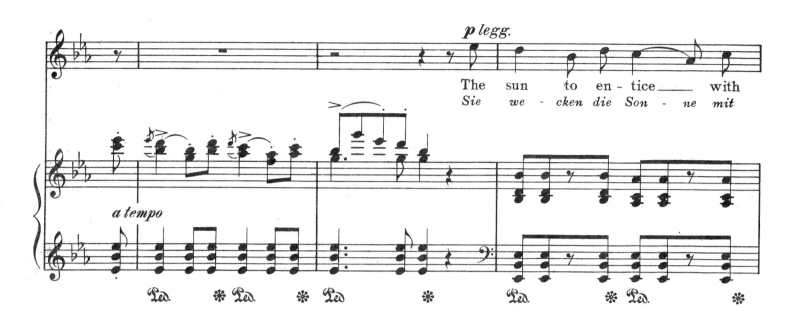

The sun to en-tice____ with
Sie we - cken die Son - ne mit

joy - -ance,
Ne - -cken,
That
den

Win - ter may cease his an - noy - ance;
Win - ter wird das____ er - schre - cken.
To start mer-ry streams in
Im Chor dann die Bäch - lein

sempre string. e cresc.

cho - rus, That scare him with song so - nor - ous; To drive him from balm - y
flie - ssen, der Sang thut ihn arg ver - drie - ssen, bald jagt ihn aus ho - hen

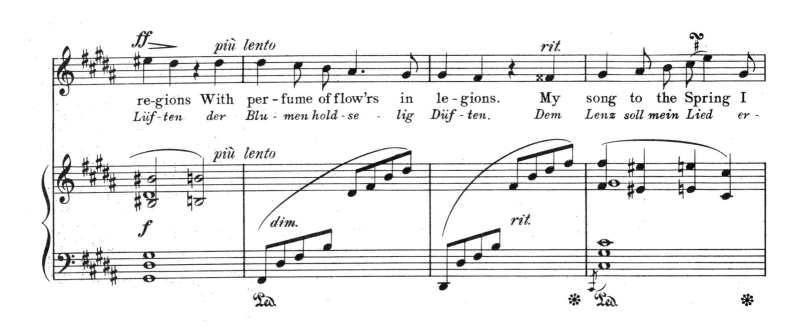

re - gions With per - fume of flow'rs in le - gions. My song to the Spring I
Lüf - ten der Blu - men hold - se - lig Düf - ten. Dem Lenz soll mein Lied er -

prof - fer.
klin - gen.

AT A YOUNG WOMAN'S BIER
(AN DER BAHRE EINER JUNGEN FRAU)

(Composed in 1873)

O. P. MONRAD *
English version by Nathan Haskell Dole
German version by Wilhelm Henzen

(Original Key)

EDVARD GRIEG, Op. 39, Nº 5

*(1849-1920)

HIDDEN LOVE
(VERBORG'NE LIEBE)

BJORNSTJERNE BJÖRNSON 1832-)*
English version by Nathan Haskell Dole
German version by Wilhelm Henzen

(Composed in 1874)

(Original Key)

EDVARD GRIEG, Op.39, №2

*d. 1910

SOLVEJG'S SONG
(SOLVEJGS LIED)

(Composed in 1874)

(Original Key)

HENRIK IBSEN (1828-1906)
English version by Arthur Westbrook
German version by W. Henzen

EDVARD GRIEG, Op. 23, №1

PIANO

The win - ter may wane and the spring-time go by, the____
Der Win - ter mag schei - den, der Früh - ling ver-gëh'n, der____

spring - time go by,_____ The sum - mer too may van - ish, the
Früh - ling ver - gëh'n,_____ der Söm - mer mag ver - wel - ken, das

year may die, the__ year may die;_____ But one day you'll re-turn, that in
Jahr ver-weh'n, das__ Jahr ver - weh'n;_____ du keh-rest mir zu-rü - cke, ge-

last I'll meet you there, at last I'll meet you there!___ Ah!___
tref - fen wir uns da, so tref - fen wir uns da!___ A ___

SOLVEJG'S SLUMBER SONG
(SOLVEJGS WIEGENLIED)

HENRIK IBSEN (1828-1906)
English version by Charles Fonteyn Manney
German version by Wilhelm Henzen

(Composed in 1875)

(Original Key)

EDVARD GRIEG, Op.23, №2

Sleep and rest, dearest
Schlaf', du theu-er-ster

boy of mine!
Kna - be mein!

I will cra-dle thee, I will watch thee.
Ich will wie-gen mein Kind und wa - chen.

A SWAN
(EIN SCHWAN)

(Composed in 1876)

(Original Key)

HENRIK IBSEN (1828-1906)
English version by Frederic Field Bullard
German version by W. Henzen

EDVARD GRIEG, Op. 25, № 2

THE FIRST PRIMROSE
(MIT EINER PRIMULA VERIS)
(Composed in 1876)

(Original Key)

J. PAULSEN (1851 -   ) *
English version by F. Corder
German version by W. Henzen

EDVARD GRIEG, Op. 26, № 4

*d. 1924

spring is love-li - er than all, The time__ of love__ and
Lenz doch ist der Won - nig - ste mit Lie - bes - lust__ und

play.____ For thee and me, O dear - est maid, The
Scherz.____ Für uns, o hol - de Maid, er - glüht der

light__ of spring is glow - ing; Then take__ the flow'r and
Früh - lings Mor - gen - son - ne; so nimm die Blum' und

rap - ture yield, Thy heart on me be - stow - ing.
gieb__ da - für dein Herz__ mit sei' - ner Won - ne.

WITH A WATER-LILY
(MIT EINER WASSERLILIE)

HENRIK IBSEN (1828-1906)
English version by Nathan Haskell Dole
German version by W. Henzen

(Composed in 1876)

(Original Key)

EDVARD GRIEG, Op. 25, No 4

a tempo — poco rit. — poco ten.

ing!——

ne.——

Child, be - ware the pond's deep stream there;
Hü - te dich, am Strom zu träu - men,

pa tempo — *poco rit.* — *poco ten.*

poco ten.

Per - il - ous it is to dream there!
furcht - bar kön - nen Flu - then schäu - men!

animato

poco ten.

poco ten.

Wa - ter-sprite pre - tends to slum - ber;
Neck ist still, als wenn er schlie - fe;

animato

mf poco ten.

poco ten. — poco rit.

Lil - ies play in count-less num - ber.
Li - lien spie - len ob der Tie - fe.

poco ten. — *poco rit.*

MINSTREL'S SONG
(SPIELMANNSLIED)

(Composed in 1876)

(Original Key, C)

HENRIK IBSEN (1828-1906)
English version by Nathan Haskell Dole
German version by W. Henzen

EDVARD GRIEG, Op. 25, № 1

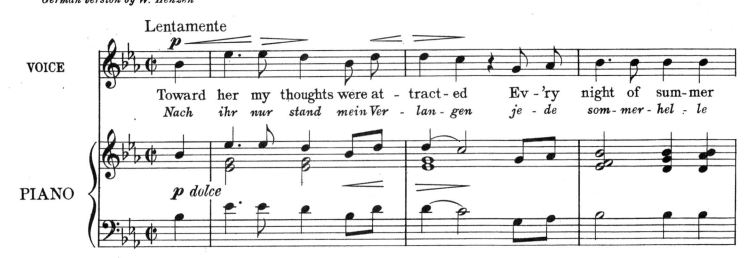

Toward her my thoughts were at - tract - ed Ev - 'ry night of sum - mer
Nach ihr nur stand mein Ver - lan - gen je - de som - mer - hel - le

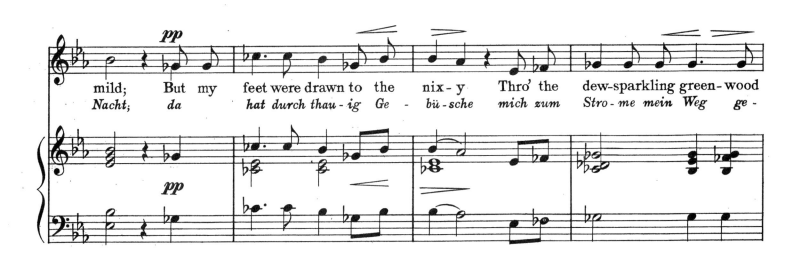

mild; But my feet were drawn to the nix - y Thro' the dew-sparkling green-wood
Nacht; da hat durch thau - ig Ge - bü - sche mich zum Stro - me mein Weg ge -

wild. Ha! know - est thou spells and mu - sic? Canst thou
bracht. Hei! kennst du Ge - sang und Schau - ern, kannst du

'TWAS ON A LOVELY EVE IN JUNE
(AM SCHÖNSTEN SOMMERABEND WAR'S)

(Composed in 1876)

(Original Key)

J. PAULSEN (1851-   )*
English version by Charles Fonteyn Manney
German version by W. Henzen

EDVARD GRIEG, Op. 26, № 2

*d. 1924

THE YOUTH
(DER BURSCH)

A. O. VINJE (1818-1870)
English version by Nathan Haskell Dole
German version by Edmund Lobedanz

(Composed in 1880)

(Original Key)

EDVARD GRIEG, Op.33, № 1

Hadst thou not been for - sak - en so, And suf - fer'd
Und wenn nicht oft be - tro - gen wär' dein Herz, so

wrong, Thou nev - er couldst have caught the flow Of love's true song.
bang, dann spräch' nicht Lie - be recht und hehr aus dei - nem Sang.

On thy life's ru - in's must thou climb, That on___ each side,
Wenn auf Ru - i - nen sich dein Sein hat auf - ge - baut,

___Thou may'st a - round thee in due time, See far and wide.
___ dann erst dein Aug', mit Bli-cken rein, weit um sich schaut.

SPRINGTIDE
(DER FRÜHLING)

(Composed in 1880)

(*Original Key*)

A. O. VINJE (1818–1880)
English version by Nathan Haskell Dole
German version by Edmund Lobedanz

EDVARD GRIEG, Op. 33, № 2

Andante espressivo

1. Now once a - gain have I
2. O - ver the hills of the
1. Ja, noch ein - mal konnt' den
2. Glit - zern - de Strah - len noch

seen spring at hand And win - ter a va - grant,
spring I could see The sun - beams a - dan - cing;
Win - ter ich seh'n dem Früh - lin - ge wei - chen,
ein - mal ich sah auf Lenz - hü - geln gau - keln,

Hed - ges and trees by the
Birds 'mid the blooms all a -
Weiss - dorn er - blüh - te mit
Schmet - ter - ling' sah ich auf

dolcissimo

south - wind were fann'd, Their blos - soms all fra - grant.
quiv - er with glee, Were gleam - ing and glan - cing.
Dol - den, so schön, so ganz oh - ne Glei - chen.
Blu - men all - da, so lu - stig sich schau - keln.

cresc. molto

ff

jew - - - el'd with flow - ers; Loud - ly a - gain chant - ed
life do I cher - ish: More has been mine than by
Blu - - - men voll Won - ne; ein - mal noch sang mir die
Glück durft' ich fin - den; mehr als ver - dient ward mir

pp

birds as of yore, For spring's_____ glad-some
mer - it I hold! And all_____ things must
Ler - che, so schön, im Som - - - - mer voll
Freu - de be - schert, und al - - - - les muss

hours.__
per - ish!
Son - ne.
schwin-den.

pp *e con Ped.*

Ped. *Ped.* *✳*

3. Once more I'll go to the spring-ver-dant vale Which glad-dens my vi-sion;
3. Ein-mal mich führt's nach dem lenz-fri-schen Thal, das Sehn-sucht mir stil-let,

Some-time I'll find there a home and shall dwell In re-gions e-lys-ian,
dort find' voll Son-ne ein Heim ich ein-mal, wo Lust mich er-fül-let.

All that by spring to the val-ley is giv'n, The flow'rs that sur-
Das, was der Lenz mir hie-nie-den ge-bar, die Blum', die ich

round me, Seem now to me like fair spir-its of heav'n And whis-per a-
pflück-te, schien mir der se-li-gen Gei-ster heh-re Schaar, der Erd' schon ent-

round me. Thus to mine ear in this birch-haunt-ed glade Does sing - ing a-
rück - te. Da - rum ich hör - te auf Schritt und auf Tritt ein räth - sel-haft

wak - en; There-fore the notes of the pipe that I made With weep -
Sin - gen, Lau - te, auf Flö - ten, die oft ich mir schnitt, wie Seuf -

- ing seem shak-en.
- zer er - klin-gen.

THE WOUNDED HEART
(DER VERWUNDETE)

(Composed in 1880)

(Original Key)

A.O. VINJE (1818-1870)
English version by Nathan Haskell Dole
German version by Edmund Lobedanz

EDVARD GRIEG, Op. 33, Nº 3

AT THE BROOKSIDE
(AN EINEM BACHE)

(Composed in 1880)

(Original Key)

A. O. VINJE (1818 – 1870)
English version by Frederic Field Bullard
German version by Edmund Lobedanz

EDVARD GRIEG, Op. 33, № 5

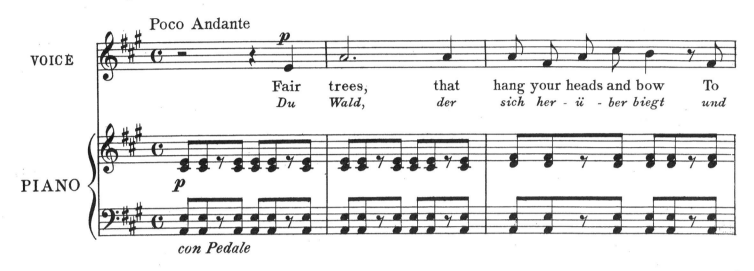

Fair   trees,   that   hang your heads and bow   To
Du   Wald,   der   sich her - ü - ber biegt   und

con Pedale

kiss the brook, so dark   and still,_____   Which un-der-mines your
küsst den schwar-zen Bach   so   still,_____   der nagt an dei - nem

roots be-low,   And to your down-fall bends its   will;_____
Mark ver-gnügt   und tief hin - un - ter zieh'n dich   will;_____

dolce

bring_____ but grief and dark de-spair,
Weh'_____ ihm bracht' und bitt' - ren Tod,

Grief _____

Weh' _____

_____ and dark de - spair._____
_____ *und bitt' - ren Tod!* _____

Fair trees!_ Fair trees!_ Fair trees! Fair trees!_____
*Du Wald!_ Du Wald!_ Du Wald! Du Wald!*_____

A VISION
(WAS ICH SAH)

(Composed in 1880)

(Original Key)

A. O. VINJE (1818-1870)
English version by Nathan Haskell Dole
German version by Max Kalbeck

EDVARD GRIEG, Op. 33, № 6

Her glan-ces so bright, De-light-ed my sight, Yet
Ach, was ich ge-sehn, und wie mir ge-schehn, das

nev-er in words could I ren-der.___ I could not por-tray, She fad-ed a-way, Why
wird nicht ge-sagt noch ge-sun-gen!___ Wohl schau' ich em-por: wann trittst du her-vor, noch

came she in my sight in – sis-tent? So daz-zling she gleam'd, Pure sun-light she seem'd, But
ein-mal, lieb-lich-ster der Ster-ne? Wann kehrst du zu-rück, mein flüch-ti-ges Glück? Zer-

dis-tant, oh, dis-tant, so dis-tant!
sto-ben, ver-weht in der Fer-ne!

THE OLD MOTHER
(DIE ALTE MUTTER)

(Composed in 1880)

A. O. VINJE (1818-1870)
English version by F. Corder
German version by Edmund Lobedanz

(Original Key)

EDVARD GRIEG, Op.33, Nº7

Thou'st wiped a-way each
Du wisch-test ab die

child-ish tear When I was sore dis-tress'd,___ And
Thrä-ne mein, war's mir im Her-zen bang,___ Und

kiss'd thy lit-tle lad-die dear, And taught him songs that
küss-test mich, den Kna-ben dein, und hauch-test in___ die

ban-ish fear From ev-'ry man-ly breast.___
Brust hin-ein den sie-ges-fro-hen Sang.___

THE ONLY THING
(DAS ERSTE)

(Composed in 1880)

(Original Key)

A. O. VINJE (1818-1870)
English version by Nathan Haskell Dole
German version by Edmund Lobedanz

EDVARD GRIEG, Op. 33, № 8

ON THE JOURNEY HOME
(AUF DER REISE ZUR HEIMATH)

A.O.VINJE (1818-1870)
English version by Nathan Haskell Dole
German version by Edmund Lobedanz

(Composed in 1880)

(Original Key)

EDVARD GRIEG, Op. 33, N.º 9

FRIENDSHIP
(EIN FREUNDSCHAFTSSTÜCK)
(Composed in 1880)

A.O. VINJE (1818-1870)
English version by Nathan Haskell Dole
German version by Edmund Lobedanz

(Original Key, D minor)

EDVARD GRIEG, Op. 33, № 10

GREETING
(GRUSS)
(Original Key)

HEINRICH HEINE (1799-1856)
English version by Charles Fonteyn Manney

EDVARD GRIEG, Op. 48, No. 1

ERE LONG, O HEART OF MINE
(DEREINST, GEDANKE MEIN)
(Original Key)

EMANUEL GEIBEL (1815-1884)
English version by Charles Fonteyn Manney

EDVARD GRIEG, Op. 48, № 2

Ere long, O heart of mine,
Der- einst, Ge- dan- kè mein,

Shall peace be thine. Tho' love's un-rest Doth still en - fold thee,
wirst ru - hig sein. Lässt Lie - bes- gluth dich still nicht wer - den,

Soon earth shall hold thee In slum - ber blest; No more to
in küh - ler Er - den da schläfst du gut; dort oh - ne

love, No more to pine,— Shall peace be thine.
Lieb' und oh - ne Pein— wirst ru - hig sein.

THE WAY OF THE WORLD
(LAUF DER WELT)

LUDWIG UHLAND (1787–1862)
English version by Charles Fonteyn Manney

(Original Key)

EDVARD GRIEG, Op.48, №3

What need of words our bliss to prove,
Wenn Lip - pe gern auf Lip - pe ruht,

When lips were join'd in ar - dent
wir hin - dern's nicht, uns dünkt es

love._____
gut._____

Young Zeph-yr woos the bud-ding rose, Nor asks if him she
Das Lüft-chen mit der Ro - se spielt, es fragt nicht: hast mich

loves; Her dew - wet_ cheek which flames and glows An_ an - sw'ring pas - sion
lieb? Das Rös - chen sich am_ Thau - e kühlt, es_ sagt nicht lan - ge:

proves. So I love her, as she loves me, Yet nei - ther says "Yes,
gieb: Ich lie - be sie, sie lie - bet mich, doch kei - nes sagt: ich

I love thee!" Yet nei - ther says "Yes, I love
lie - be dich! doch kei - nes sagt: ich lie - be

poco rit.

(senza cresc.)

thee!"
dich!

a tempo

poco rit.

pp

THE SILENT NIGHTINGALE
(DIE VERSCHWIEGENE NACHTIGALL)

(Original Key)

WALTHER von der VOGELWEIDE (died about 1227)
English version by Nathan Haskell Dole

EDVARD GRIEG, Op 48, № 4

Allegretto *(sempre con mezza voce)*

VOICE

PIANO

dolce
pp

p

Where with my lov - er,
Un - ter den Lin - den,

poco cresc.

On___ the heath - er, 'Neath fra - grant lin - dens did___ I
an___ der Hai - de, wo ich mit mei - nem Trau - ten

poco cresc.

stay, You might dis - cov - er How___ to - geth - er___ The
sass, da mögt ihr fin - den, wie___ wir Bei - de die

grass___ and flow'rs___ all bro - ken lay!
Blu - men bra - - - - chen und das___ Gras.

IN TIME OF ROSES
(ZUR ROSENZEIT)
(Original Key)

JOHANN WOLFGANG von GOETHE (1749-1832)
English version by Charles Fonteyn Manney

EDVARD GRIEG, Op. 48, № 5

Allegretto serioso

VOICE

PIANO

con Pedale

Love-ly ro - ses, are ye fad - ed,
Ihr ver - blü - het, sü - sse Ro - sen,

Ne'er up - on her bos - om borne? Bloom for me whose hope is
mei - ne Lie - be trug euch nicht; blü - het, ach! dem Hoff - nungs -

poco ten.

shad - ed, And whose soul with grief is torn!
lo - sen, dem der Gram die See - le bricht!

p poco più mosso *cresc.* *f*

Sad - ly now my thoughts are turn - ing To the days when
Je - ner Ta - ge denk' ich trau - ernd als ich, En - gel,

poco più mosso

p *cresc.* *f*

you___ were kind;
an___ dir hing,

When for you I pluck'd at
auf das er - ste Knösp - chen

morn - ing
lau - ernd,

The first rose - buds I___ could find;
früh zu mei - nem Gar - ten ging;

Ev-'ry flow - 'ret,
al - le Blü - then,

fruits the rar - est
al - le Früch - te

Glad - ly to your
noch___ zu dei - nen

feet I bore,
Fü - ssen trug,

While I sought in eyes the dear - est
und vor dei - nem An - ge - sich - te

poco a poco meno mosso e dim.

A DREAM
(EIN TRAUM)

(Original Key)

FRIEDRICH von BODENSTEDT (1819-1892)
English version by Charles Fonteyn Manney

EDVARD GRIEG, Op. 48, № 6

*) very softly

We heard the dis - tant vil - lage chime;
*fern aus dem Dor - fe scholl Ge - läut'_*

In ev -'ry look our
wir wa - ren gan - zer

rap - ture glow'd,
Won - ne voll,

Our hearts were held in bliss sub-lime.
ver - sun - ken ganz in Se - lig-keit.

That gold-en dream____ was not so fair____
Und schö - ner noch,____ als einst der Traum,____

____ As wak-ing joys im - part - ed there:
____ be - gab es sich in Wirk - lich-keit:

A - gain we stood____
es war im grü -

cresc.

in for-est glade,_____ Where spring had spread her ver-dant shade;
_- nen Wal - des - raum,_____ es war zur war - men Früh-lings-zeit,_

cresc.

p _poco a poco stringendo e cresc._

The stream-let flow'd, the wood - bird sang, A sound of bells the
der Wald - bach schwoll, die Knos - pe sprang, Ge - läut' er-scholl vom

p _poco a poco stringendo e cresc._

breez _-_ es bore; _____ I held thee fast,
_Dor - fe her: _____ Ich hielt dich fest,_

I held thee long, And I shall leave thee nev - er - more! _____
_ich hielt dich lang und las - se dich nun nim - mer - mehr! _____

THE MOTHER SINGS
(DIE MUTTER SINGT)

VILHELM KRAG (1871-   )*
English version by Nathan Haskell Dole

(Original Key, Eb minor)

EDVARD GRIEG, Op. 60, No 2

Gret-chen lies in her cof - fin, Deep in the dark, dark mould.___ There's the hood that I gave her, Lined with___ red, red gold.

Irm - lein ru - het im Sar - ge tief in dem dun - klen Grab,___ nahm ihr sei - den - es Häub - chen mit in die Gruft hin - ab.

Down in her nar - row cof - fin

Tief in die schwar - ze Er - de

*d. 1933

My lit - tle maid's at rest; Cold, her small hands are fold - ed
senkt' ich mein Ir - me - lein, fal - te - te die kal - ten Händ - chen

O - ver her qui - et breast. Lone - ly at night I am
ü - ber dem wei - ssen Lein. Ein - sam nun träum' ich die

sit - ting, While on the bay tem-pests rave,___ Tear - ing all of the
Nacht hin, die Stür - me, sie gehn ü - ber's Meer,___ streu - en al - le die

blos - soms From lit - tle Gret - chen's grave.
Blu - men von Irm - lein's Grab um - her.

IN THE BOAT
(IM KAHNE)
(Original Key)

VILHELM KRAG (1871-) *
English version by Nathan Haskell Dole

EDVARD GRIEG, Op. 60, № 3

Sea - gulls, ' sea - gulls with plum - age snow - y!
Mö - ven, ' Mö - ven in wei - ssen Flo - - cken! '

Sun - light gay!
Son - nen - schein!

Gos - lings with yel - low
En - ten stol - zie - ren in

stock-ings show-y Strut a - way.
gel - ben So - cken schmuck und fein.

Row, row to is-lands fair,
Fahr; fahr' zum Fi-scher-strand,

*d. 1933

Then will we dance thro' the bright-ly shin-ing Warm June night.
Dann lass uns tan - zen die war - me, lich - te Ju - ni - nacht.

Wait, wait! Mid-
Wart', wart', zu

un poco rit.

a tempo

dolce
a tempo

anim.

sum-mer-tide   Soon will make thee my   hap-py bride,   ⋁ All of the fid-dle-bows   fly-ing.
Sank-te Hans   giebt es Hoch-zeit mit   lust'-gem Tanz,   ⋁ Gei-gen in Hül-le und   Fül-le.

anim.

p poco rit. a tempo

"Fair my__ la-dy."
Wo - wo - wil - le.

tranq.

a tempo

pp

poco rit.

p

simili

Rock me,   rock me, O wave so   ten - der, On__ the tide!
Wie - ge ,   wie - ge mich, blan - ke   Wel - le, im - mer - fort!

THE MOUNTAIN MAID
(DAS KIND DER BERGE)

(Composed in 1898)

(Original Key, E minor)

ARNE GARBORG (1851-   ) *
English version by Arthur Westbrook
German version by Eugen von Enzberg

EDVARD GRIEG, Op.67, No 2

*d. 1924

bear - ing, her voice,____ her look____ A strange, mourn-ful calm dis-
bär - de Mie - ne und Wort____ ver - räth die - se düst - 're

close, mourn-ful calm dis - close.____ 'Neath the
Ruh', die - se düst - 're Ruh'!____ Un - ter'm

lus - trous gloom of her hair, Shine her eyes with a haunt - ing
dun - keln lo - cki - gen Haar strahlt das Au ge mit mat - tem

gleam; Some____ world that we know not she sees____ Re -
Schein; sie____ starrt wie im Traum vor sich hin____ in

THE TRYST
(STELLDICHEIN)
(Composed in 1898)

(Original Key)

ARNE GARBORG (1851-)*
English version by Charles Fonteyn Manney
German version by Eugen von Enzberg

EDVARD GRIEG, Op. 67, № 4

*d. 1924

molto rit. *ff a tempo*

to meet her glad-ly rush - es.
da kommt er ja ge-gan - gen.

molto rit. animato a tempo

a tempo

She fain would flee from out the for - est glade,___ But
Fort will sie flie-hen in die Heid' hin - aus,___ doch

bonds of mag-ic to the spot en - chain her,
ist's, als ob ein Zauber fest sie bän - de;
His hands so warm-ly clasp-ing hers re-
sie rei-chen Bei - de sich die war-men

p dolce

strain her, And so they stand, and ne'er a word is said.
Hän - de und steh'n so da, und wis-sen kei-nen Rath.

LOVE
(LIEBE)

(Composed in 1898)

(Original Key)

ARNE GARBORG (1851-)*
English version by Charles Fontcyn Manney
German version by Eugen von Enzberg

EDVARD GRIEG, Op. 67, No 5

*d. 1924

hands till the blood is flow-ing! Oh, come and hold me so close to thee That sun and
bind', bis die Hän-de blu-ten! O komm und press' mich so fest an dich, dass Mond und

moon I no long-er see! _____ Is there no mag-ic the pow'r pos-sess-es To guide me
Son-ne ver-geht für mich! _____ O könnt' durch Zau-ber es mir ge-lin-gen, so würd' ich

straight to thy soul's re-cess-es? I'd en-ter deep to thy deep-est heart, And nev-er
tief in dein Her-ze drin-gen, ich wür-de drin-gen gar tief hin-ein und wei-len

dwell from my love a-part! _____ O thou, whose im-age my mind is
ein-zig beim Lieb-sten mein! _____ O du, der woh-net im Her-zen

L'istesso tempo

AT MOTHER'S GRAVE
(AM GRABE DER MUTTER)

(Composed in 1900)

(Original Key)

OTTO BENZON *
English version by Nathan Haskell Dole
German version by Hans Schmidt

EDVARD GRIEG, Op. 69, №3

Calm - ly sleep, O moth - er blest,
Schla - fe süss, lieb Müt - ter - lein,

Sleep the sleep that has no dream - ing; Heed - less how our
schlaf' im stil - len Sar ge drin - nen, schwe - re, ban ge

tears are stream-ing As we lay thee in earth's breast.
Thrä - nen rin - nen nie - der auf den dunk - len Schrein.

*(1856-1927)

DREAMS
(TRÄUME)

(Composed in 1900)

(Original Key)

OTTO BENZON *
English version by Nathan Haskell Dole
German version by Hans Schmidt

EDVARD GRIEG, Op. 69, N₉ 5

You're all that I treas - ure, my
Du warst mir mein Al - les, das

dear - est de - light,___ My care and my glad - ness, by day and by
reich mich ge - macht,___ mein Sor - gen, mein Freu - en bei Tag und bei

night.___ You fill all my mind, you en-
Nacht.___ Du füll - test die See - le mit

*(1856-1927)

harsh dis - il - lu - sion o'er-whelm'd me with grief!
Wirk - lich - keit Stren - ge mich rauh draus ver - stiess.

pp

An - oth - er than I by your love you have crown'd,
Nicht mir war be - schie - den dein Herz, dei - ne Hand,
Now morning is
es grau - te der

pp un poco rall.

dawn - ing the dreams false are found.
Mor - gen, das Traum - bild ent - schwand.

Tempo I
p

ffz un poco rall.

Fare-well, then, ye vis - ions that quick - en my care!___ Fare-
Fahrt wohl denn, ihr Träu - me, die reich mich ge - macht,___ die

p

pp

EROS

(Original Key)

OTTO BENZON*
English version by Nathan Haskell Dole
German version by Hans Schmidt

EDVARD GRIEG, Op. 70, № 1

Hear me, ye north-ern-born hearts, cold as snow,
Hört mich, ihr fro-sti-gen Her-zen im Nord,

Ye who seek peace in re-
ihr, die ihr Glück im Ent-

noun-cing re-sign'd-ly,
sa-gen wollt fin-den,

Ye wan-der blind-ly, ye wan-der blind-ly,
weh' euch, ihr Blin-den, weh' euch, ihr Blin-den,

*(1856-1927)

Cher - ish her who is whol - ly thine own,
Hal - tet um - fasst sie, die ganz___ sich euch giebt,

Cher - ish the one___ thou lov - est a - lone!
stark, wie die Ju - gend ein - zig nur liebt,

stretto e cresc. poco a poco

Love thy dar - ling ⌄ with all the fire, ⌄ All of life's deep
hal - tet um - fasst sie, ⌄ mit all' der Gluth, ⌄ all' der Kraft der

lim - it - less long-ing, ⌄ Which in thy fast - beat-ing heart___ must glow. ⌄
flam - men - den See - le, ⌄ die hoch das Herz euch in Se - lig-keit schwellt, ⌄

RADIANT NIGHT
(LICHTE NACHT)
(Original Key)

OTTO BENZON *
English version by Nathan Haskell Dole
German version by Hans Schmidt

EDVARD GRIEG, Op. 70, № 3

*(1856-1927)

TAKE GOOD HEED
(SIEH' DICH VOR)
(Original Key)

OTTO BENZON*

English version by Nathan Haskell Dole
German version by Hans Schmidt

EDVARD GRIEG, Op. 70, № 4

Take good heed where thou choos-est thy way, Oft the road cross-es
mi-ry mo-rass-es; Run no chance on the brink to stay, Paths that one knows, there one
pass-es. Oft in sor-row ends mer-riest play: Take good heed where thou choos-est thy

Sieh' dich vor, eh' du wählst dei-nen Weg, man-cher Pfad führt hin-
aus in die Wei-te, ei-ner nur ist der si-che-re Steg, der an das Ziel dich ge-
lei-te. Rings-um dräu-en Ge-strüpp und Ge-heg; sieh' dich vor, eh' du wählst dei-nen

way.
Weg!

Take good heed where thou set-test thy foot!
Sieh' dich vor, eh' du se-tzest den Fuss,

Look out well where paths are the clean-est;
dass die rich-ti-ge Bahn er be-schrei-te,

Fate be-tides thee a Dead Sea fruit
fes-ten Bo-den be-tre-ten er muss,

If 'gainst thine own self thou sin-nest!
dass er nicht strau-ch'le noch glei-te.

Bit-ter rue has a sin at its root:
Sonst zu spät kom-men Reu' dir und Buss',

Take good heed where thou set-test thy foot.
sieh' dich vor, eh' du se-tzest den Fuss!

Dover Opera, Choral and Lieder Scores

Bach, Johann Sebastian, ELEVEN GREAT CANTATAS. Full vocal-instrumental score from Bach-Gesellschaft edition. *Christ lag in Todesbanden, Ich hatte viel Bekümmerniss, Jauchhzet Gott in allen Landen,* eight others. Study score. 350pp. 9 x 12. 23268-9

Bach, Johann Sebastian, MASS IN B MINOR IN FULL SCORE. The crowning glory of Bach's lifework in the field of sacred music and a universal statement of Christian faith, reprinted from the authoritative Bach-Gesellschaft edition. Translation of texts. 320pp. 9 x 12. 25992-7

Bach, Johann Sebastian, SEVEN GREAT SACRED CANTATAS IN FULL SCORE. Seven favorite sacred cantatas. Printed from a clear, modern engraving and sturdily bound; new literal line-for-line translations. Reliable Bach-Gesellschaft edition. Complete German texts. 256pp. 9 x 12. 24950-6

Bach, Johann Sebastian, SIX GREAT SECULAR CANTATAS IN FULL SCORE. Bach's nearest approach to comic opera. *Hunting Cantata, Wedding Cantata, Aeolus Appeased, Phoebus and Pan, Coffee Cantata,* and *Peasant Cantata.* 286pp. 9 x 12. 23934-9

Beethoven, Ludwig van, FIDELIO IN FULL SCORE. Beethoven's only opera, complete in one affordable volume, including all spoken German dialogue. Republication of C. F. Peters, Leipzig edition. 272pp. 9 x 12. 24740-6

Beethoven, Ludwig van, SONGS FOR SOLO VOICE AND PIANO. 71 lieder, including "Adelaide," "Wonne der Wehmuth," "Die ehre Gottes aus der Natur," and famous cycle *An die ferne Geliebta.* Breitkopf & Härtel edition. 192pp. 9 x 12. 25125-X

Bizet, Georges, CARMEN IN FULL SCORE. Complete, authoritative score of perhaps the world's most popular opera, in the version most commonly performed today, with recitatives by Ernest Guiraud. 574pp. 9 x 12. 25820-3

Brahms, Johannes, COMPLETE SONGS FOR SOLO VOICE AND PIANO (two volumes). A total of 113 songs in complete score by greatest lieder writer since Schubert. Series I contains 15-song cycle *Die Schone Magelone*; Series II includes famous "Lullaby." Total of 448pp. 9⅜ x 12¼.
Series I: 23820-2
Series II: 23821-0

Brahms, Johannes, COMPLETE SONGS FOR SOLO VOICE AND PIANO: Series III. 64 songs, published from 1877 to 1886, include such favorites as "Geheimnis," "Alte Liebe," and "Vergebliches Standchen." 224pp. 9 x 12. 23822-9

Brahms, Johannes, COMPLETE SONGS FOR SOLO VOICE AND PIANO: Series IV. 120 songs that complete the Brahms song oeuvre, with sensitive arrangements of 91 folk and traditional songs. 240pp. 9 x 12. 23823-7

Brahms, Johannes, GERMAN REQUIEM IN FULL SCORE. Definitive Breitkopf & Härtel edition of Brahms's greatest vocal work, fully scored for solo voices, mixed chorus and orchestra. 208pp. 9⅜ x 12¼. 25486-0

Debussy, Claude, PELLÉAS ET MÉLISANDE IN FULL SCORE. Reprinted from the E. Fromont (1904) edition, this volume faithfully reproduces the full orchestral-vocal score of Debussy's sole and enduring opera masterpiece. 416pp. 9 x 12. (Available in U.S. only) 24825-9

Debussy, Claude, SONGS, 1880–1904. Rich selection of 36 songs set to texts by Verlaine, Baudelaire, Pierre Louÿs, Charles d'Orleans, others. 175pp. 9 x 12. 24131-9

Fauré, Gabriel, SIXTY SONGS. "Clair de lune," "Apres un reve," "Chanson du pecheur," "Automne," and other great songs set for medium voice. Reprinted from French editions. 288pp. 8⅜ x 11. (Not available in France or Germany) 26534-X

Gilbert, W. S. and Sullivan, Sir Arthur, THE AUTHENTIC GILBERT & SULLIVAN SONGBOOK, 92 songs, uncut, original keys, in piano renderings approved by Sullivan. 399pp. 9 x 12. 23482-7

Gilbert, W. S. and Sullivan, Sir Arthur, HMS PINAFORE IN FULL SCORE. New edition by Carl Simpson and Ephraim Hammett Jones. Some of Gilbert's most clever flashes of wit and a number of Sullivan's most charming melodies in a handsome, authoritative new edition based on original manuscripts and early sources. 256pp. 9 x 12. 42201-1

Gilbert, W. S. and Sullivan, Sir Arthur (Carl Simpson and Ephraim Hammett Jones, eds.), THE PIRATES OF PENZANCE IN FULL SCORE. New performing edition corrects numerous errors, offers performers the choice of two versions of the Act II finale, and gives the first accurate full score of the "Climbing over Rocky Mountain" section. 288pp. 9 x 12. 41891-X

Hale, Philip (ed.), FRENCH ART SONGS OF THE NINETEENTH CENTURY: 39 Works from Berlioz to Debussy. 39 songs from romantic period by 18 composers: Berlioz, Chausson, Debussy (six songs), Gounod, Massenet, Thomas, etc. French text, English singing translation for high voice. 182pp. 9 x 12. (Not available in France or Germany) 23680-3

Handel, George Frideric, GIULIO CESARE IN FULL SCORE. Great Baroque masterpiece reproduced directly from authoritative Deutsche Handelgesellschaft edition. Gorgeous melodies, inspired orchestration. Complete and unabridged. 160pp. 9⅜ x 12¼. 25056-3

Handel, George Frideric, MESSIAH IN FULL SCORE. An authoritative full-score edition of the oratorio that is the best-known, most-beloved, most-performed large-scale musical work in the English-speaking world. 240pp. 9 x 12. 26067-4

Lehar, Franz, THE MERRY WIDOW: Complete Score for Piano and Voice in English. Complete score for piano and voice, reprinted directly from the first English translation (1907) published by Chappell & Co., London. 224pp. 8⅜ x 11¼. (Available in U.S. only) 24514-4

Liszt, Franz, THIRTY SONGS. Selection of extremely worthwhile though not widely-known songs. Texts in French, German, and Italian, all with English translations. Piano, high voice. 144pp. 9 x 12. 23197-6

Monteverdi, Claudio, MADRIGALS: BOOK IV & V. 39 finest madrigals with new line-for-line literal English translations of the poems facing the Italian text. 256pp. 8⅛ x 11. (Available in U.S. only) 25102-0

Moussorgsky, Modest Petrovich, BORIS GODUNOV IN FULL SCORE (Rimsky-Korsakov Version). Russian operatic masterwork in most-recorded, most-performed version. Authoritative Moscow edition. 784pp. 8⅜ x 11¼. 25321-X

Mozart, Wolfgang Amadeus, THE ABDUCTION FROM THE SERAGLIO IN FULL SCORE. Mozart's early comic masterpiece, exactingly reproduced from the authoritative Breitkopf & Härtel edition. 320pp. 9 x 12. 26004-6

Mozart, Wolfgang Amadeus, COSI FAN TUTTE IN FULL SCORE. Scholarly edition of one of Mozart's greatest operas. Da Ponte libretto. Commentary. Preface. Translated Front Matter. 448pp. 9⅜ x 12¼. (Available in U.S. only) 24528-4

Available from your music dealer or write for ***free*** *Music Catalog to*
Dover Publications, Inc., Dept. MUBI, 31 East 2nd Street, Mineola, NY 11501
Visit us online at ***www.doverpublications.com***

Dover Opera, Choral and Lieder Scores

Mozart, Wolfgang Amadeus, DON GIOVANNI: COMPLETE ORCHESTRAL SCORE. Full score that contains everything from the original version, along with later arias, recitatives, and duets added to original score for Vienna performance. Peters edition. Study score. 468pp. 9⅜ x 12¼. (Available in U.S. only) 23026-0

Mozart, Wolfgang Amadeus, THE MAGIC FLUTE (DIE ZAUBERFLÖTE) IN FULL SCORE. Authoritative C. F. Peters edition of Mozart's brilliant last opera still widely popular. Includes all the spoken dialogue. 226pp. 9 x 12. 24783-X

Mozart, Wolfgang Amadeus, THE MARRIAGE OF FIGARO: COMPLETE SCORE. Finest comic opera ever written. Full score, beautifully engraved, includes passages often cut in other editions. Peters edition. Study score. 448pp. 9⅜ x 12¼. (Available in U.S. only) 23751-6

Mozart, Wolfgang Amadeus, REQUIEM IN FULL SCORE. Masterpiece of vocal composition, among the most recorded and performed works in the repertoire. Authoritative edition published by Breitkopf & Härtel, Wiesbaden. 203pp. 8⅜ x 11¼. 25311-2

Offenbach, Jacques, OFFENBACH'S SONGS FROM THE GREAT OPERETTAS. Piano, vocal (French text) for 38 most popular songs: *Orphée, Belle Héléne, Vie Parisienne, Duchesse de Gérolstein,* others. 21 illustrations. 195pp. 9 x 12. 23341-3

Puccini, Giacomo, LA BOHÈME IN FULL SCORE. Authoritative Italian edition of one of the world's most beloved operas. English translations of list of characters and instruments. 416pp. 8⅜ x 11¼. (Not available in United Kingdom, France, Germany or Italy) 25477-1

Rossini, Gioacchino, THE BARBER OF SEVILLE IN FULL SCORE. One of the greatest comic operas ever written, reproduced here directly from the authoritative score published by Ricordi. 464pp. 8⅜ x 11¼. 26019-4

Schubert, Franz, COMPLETE SONG CYCLES. Complete piano, vocal music of *Die Schöne Müllerin, Die Winterreise, Schwanengesang.* Also Drinker English singing translations. Breitkopf & Härtel edition. 217pp. 9⅜ x 12¼. 22649-2

Schubert, Franz, SCHUBERT'S SONGS TO TEXTS BY GOETHE. Only one-volume edition of Schubert's Goethe songs from authoritative Breitkopf & Härtel edition, plus all revised versions. New prose translation of poems. 84 songs. 256pp. 9⅜ x 12¼. 23752-4

Schubert, Franz, 59 FAVORITE SONGS. "Der Wanderer," "Ave Maria," "Hark, Hark, the Lark," and 56 other masterpieces of lieder reproduced from the Breitkopf & Härtel edition. 256pp. 9⅜ x 12¼. 24849-6

Schumann, Robert, SELECTED SONGS FOR SOLO VOICE AND PIANO. Over 100 of Schumann's greatest lieder, set to poems by Heine, Goethe, Byron, others. Breitkopf & Härtel edition. 248pp. 9⅜ x 12¼. 24202-1

Strauss, Richard, DER ROSENKAVALIER IN FULL SCORE. First inexpensive edition of great operatic masterpiece, reprinted complete and unabridged from rare, limited Fürstner edition (1910) approved by Strauss. 528pp. 9⅜ x 12¼. (Available in U.S. only) 25498-4

Strauss, Richard, DER ROSENKAVALIER: VOCAL SCORE. Inexpensive edition reprinted directly from original Fürstner (1911) edition of vocal score. Verbal text, vocal line and piano "reduction." 448pp. 8⅜ x 11¼. (Not available in Europe or the United Kingdom) 25501-8

Strauss, Richard, SALOME IN FULL SCORE. Atmospheric color predominates in composer's first great operatic success. Definitive Fürstner score, now extremely rare. 352pp. 9⅜ x 12¼. (Available in U.S. only) 24208-0

Verdi, Giuseppe, AÏDA IN FULL SCORE. Verdi's glorious, most popular opera, reprinted from an authoritative edition published by G. Ricordi, Milan. 448pp. 9 x 12. 26172-7

Verdi, Giuseppe, FALSTAFF. Verdi's last great work, his first and only comedy. Complete unabridged score from original Ricordi edition. 480pp. 8⅜ x 11¼. 24017-7

Verdi, Giuseppe, OTELLO IN FULL SCORE. The penultimate Verdi opera, his tragic masterpiece. Complete unabridged score from authoritative Ricordi edition, with Front Matter translated. 576pp. 8¼ x 11. 25040-7

Verdi, Giuseppe, REQUIEM IN FULL SCORE. Immensely popular with choral groups and music lovers. Republication of edition published by C. F. Peters, Leipzig. Study score. 204pp. 9⅜ x 12¼. (Available in U.S. only) 23682-X

Wagner, Richard, DAS RHEINGOLD IN FULL SCORE. Complete score, clearly reproduced from B. Schott's authoritative edition. New translation of German Front Matter. 328pp. 9 x 12. 24925-5

Wagner, Richard, DIE MEISTERSINGER VON NÜRNBERG. Landmark in history of opera, in complete vocal and orchestral score of one of the greatest comic operas. C. F. Peters edition, Leipzig. Study score. 823pp. 8⅛ x 11. 23276-X

Wagner, Richard, DIE WALKÜRE. Complete orchestral score of the most popular of the operas in the Ring Cycle. Reprint of the edition published in Leipzig by C. F. Peters, ca. 1910. Study score. 710pp. 8⅜ x 11¼. 23566-1

Wagner, Richard, THE FLYING DUTCHMAN IN FULL SCORE. Great early masterpiece reproduced directly from limited Weingartner edition (1896), incorporating Wagner's revisions. Text, stage directions in English, German, Italian. 432pp. 9⅜ x 12¼. 25629-4

Wagner, Richard, GÖTTERDÄMMERUNG. Full operatic score, first time available in U.S. Reprinted directly from rare 1877 first edition. 615pp. 9⅜ x 12¼. 24250-1

Wagner, Richard, LOHENGRIN IN FULL SCORE. Wagner's most accessible opera. Reproduced from first engraved edition (Breitkopf & Härtel, 1887). 295pp. 9⅜ x 12¼. 24335-4

Wagner, Richard, PARSIFAL IN FULL SCORE. Composer's deeply personal treatment of the legend of the Holy Grail, renowned for splendid music, glowing orchestration. C. F. Peters edition. 592pp. 8⅛ x 11. 25175-6

Wagner, Richard, SIEGFRIED IN FULL SCORE. *Siegfried,* third opera of Wagner's famous Ring Cycle, is reproduced from first edition (1876). 439pp. 9⅜ x 12¼. 24456-3

Wagner, Richard, TANNHAUSER IN FULL SCORE. Reproduces the original 1845 full orchestral and vocal score as slightly amended in 1847. Included is the ballet music for Act I written for the 1861 Paris production. 576pp. 8⅜ x 11¼. 24649-3

Wagner, Richard, TRISTAN UND ISOLDE. Full orchestral score with complete instrumentation. Study score. 655pp. 8⅛ x 11. 22915-7

von Weber, Carl Maria, DER FREISCHÜTZ. Full orchestral score to first Romantic opera, forerunner to Wagner and later developments. Still very popular. Study score, including full spoken text. 203pp. 9 x 12. 23449-5

Wolf, Hugo, THE COMPLETE MÖRIKE SONGS. Splendid settings to music of 53 German poems by Eduard Mörike, including "Der Tambour," "Elfenlied," and "Verborganheit." New prose translations. 208pp. 9⅜ x 12¼. 24380-X

Wolf, Hugo, SPANISH AND ITALIAN SONGBOOKS. Total of 90 songs by great 19th-century master of the genre. Reprint of authoritative C. F. Peters edition. New Translations of German texts. 256pp. 9⅜ x 12¼. 26156-5

Available from your music dealer or write for ***free*** *Music Catalog to*
Dover Publications, Inc., Dept. MUBI, 31 East 2nd Street, Mineola, NY 11501
Visit us online at ***www.doverpublications.com***

Dover Popular Songbooks

(Arranged by title)

ALEXANDER'S RAGTIME BAND AND OTHER FAVORITE SONG HITS, 1901–1911, David A. Jasen (ed.). Fifty vintage popular songs America still sings, reprinted in their entirety from the original editions. Introduction. 224pp. 9 x 12. (Available in U.S. only) 25331-7

AMERICAN BALLADS AND FOLK SONGS, John A. Lomax and Alan Lomax. Over 200 songs, music and lyrics: "Frankie and Albert," "John Henry," "Frog Went a-Courtin'," "Down in the Valley," "Skip to My Lou," other favorites. Notes on each song. 672pp. 5⅜ x 8½. 28276-7

AMERICAN FOLK SONGS FOR GUITAR, David Nadal (ed.). Forty-nine classics for beginning and intermediate guitar players, including "Beautiful Dreamer," "Amazing Grace," "Aura Lee," "John Henry," "The Gift to Be Simple," "Go Down, Moses," "Sweet Betsy from Pike," "Short'nin Bread," many more. 96pp. 9 x 12. 41700-X

THE AMERICAN SONG TREASURY: 100 Favorites, Theodore Raph (ed.). Complete piano arrangements, guitar chords, and lyrics for 100 best-loved tunes, "Buffalo Gals," "Oh, Suzanna," "Clementine," "Camptown Races," and much more. 416pp. 8¼ x 11. 25222-1

"BEALE STREET" AND OTHER CLASSIC BLUES: 38 Works, 1901–1921, David A. Jasen (ed.). "St. Louis Blues," "The Hesitating Blues," "Down Home Blues," "Jelly Roll Blues," "Railroad Blues," and many more. Reproduced directly from rare sheet music (including original covers). Introduction. 160pp. 9 x 12. (Available in U.S. only) 40183-9

THE CIVIL WAR SONGBOOK, Richard Crawford (ed.). 37 songs: "Battle Hymn of the Republic," "Drummer Boy of Shiloh," "Dixie," and 34 more. 157pp. 9 x 12. 23422-3

CIVIL WAR SONGS AND BALLADS FOR GUITAR, Compiled, Edited, and Arranged by Jerry Silverman. 41 favorites, among them "Marching Through Georgia," "The Battle Hymn of the Republic," "Tenting on the Old Camp Ground," and "When Johnny Comes Marching Home." 160pp. 9 x 12. 41902-9

FAVORITE CHRISTMAS CAROLS, selected and arranged by Charles J. F. Cofone. Title, music, first verse and refrain of 34 traditional carols in handsome calligraphy; also subsequent verses and other information in type. 79pp. 8⅜ x 11. 20445-6

FAVORITE SONGS OF THE NINETIES, Robert Fremont (ed.). 88 favorites: "Ta-Ra-Ra-Boom-De-Aye," "The Band Played on," "Bird in a Gilded Cage," etc. 401pp. 9 x 12. 21536-9

500 BEST-LOVED SONG LYRICS, Ronald Herder (ed.). Complete lyrics for well-known folk songs, hymns, popular and show tunes, more. "Oh Susanna," "The Battle Hymn of the Republic," "When Johnny Comes Marching Home," hundreds more. Indispensable for singalongs, parties, family get-togethers, etc. 416pp. 5⅜ x 8½. 29725-X

"FOR ME AND MY GAL" AND OTHER FAVORITE SONG HITS, 1915–1917, David A. Jasen (ed.). 31 great hits: Pretty Baby, MacNamara's Band, Over There, Old Grey Mare, Beale Street, M-O-T-H-E-R, more, with original sheet music covers, complete vocal and piano. 144pp. 9 x 12. 28127-2

MY FIRST BOOK OF AMERICAN FOLK SONGS: 20 Favorite Pieces in Easy Piano Arrangements, Bergerac (ed.). Expert settings of traditional favorites by a well-known composer and arranger for young pianists: *Amazing Grace, Blue Tail Fly, Sweet Betsy from Pike,* many more. 48pp. 8¼ x 11. 28885-4

MY FIRST BOOK OF CHRISTMAS SONGS: 20 Favorite Songs in Easy Piano Arrangements, Bergerac (ed.). Beginners will love playing these beloved favorites in easy arrangements: "Jingle Bells," "Deck the Halls," "Joy to the World," "Silent Night," "Away in a Manger," "Hark! The Herald Angels Sing," 14 more. Illustrations. 48pp. 8¼ x 11. 29718-7

ONE HUNDRED ENGLISH FOLKSONGS, Cecil J. Sharp (ed.). Border ballads, folksongs, collected from all over Great Britain. "Lord Bateman," "Henry Martin," "The Green Wedding," many others. Piano. 235pp. 9 x 12. 23192-5

"PEG O' MY HEART" AND OTHER FAVORITE SONG HITS, 1912 & 1913, Stanley Appelbaum (ed.). 36 songs by Berlin, Herbert, Handy and others, with complete lyrics, full piano arrangements and original sheet music covers in black and white. 176pp. 9 x 12. 25998-6

POPULAR IRISH SONGS, Florence Leniston (ed.). 37 all-time favorites with vocal and piano arrangements: "My Wild Irish Rose," "Irish Eyes are Smiling," "Last Rose of Summer," "Danny Boy," many more. 160pp. 26755-5

"A PRETTY GIRL IS LIKE A MELODY" AND OTHER FAVORITE SONG HITS, 1918–1919, David A. Jasen (ed.). "After You've Gone," "How Ya Gonna Keep 'Em Down on the Farm," "I'm Always Chasing Rainbows," "Rock-a-Bye Your Baby" and 36 other Golden Oldies. 176pp. 9 x 12. 29421-8

A RUSSIAN SONG BOOK, Rose N. Rubin and Michael Stillman (eds.). 25 traditional folk songs, plus 19 popular songs by twentieth-century composers. Full piano arrangements, guitar chords. Lyrics in original Cyrillic, transliteration and English translation. With discography. 112pp. 9 x 12. 26118-2

"THE ST. LOUIS BLUES" AND OTHER SONG HITS OF 1914, Sandy Marrone (ed.). Full vocal and piano for "By the Beautiful Sea," "Play a Simple Melody," "They Didn't Believe Me,"–21 songs in all. 112pp. 9 x 12. 26383-5

SEVENTY SCOTTISH SONGS, Helen Hopekirk (ed.). Complete piano and vocals for classics of Scottish song: *Flow Gently, Sweet Afton, Comin' thro' the Rye (Gin a Body Meet a Body), The Campbells are Comin', Robin Adair,* many more. 208pp. 8⅜ x 11. 27029-7

SONGS OF THE CIVIL WAR, Irwin Silber (ed.). Piano, vocal, guitar chords for 125 songs including "Battle Cry of Freedom," "Marching Through Georgia," "Dixie," "Oh, I'm a Good Old Rebel," "The Drummer Boy of Shiloh," many more. 400pp. 8⅜ x 11. 28438-7

STEPHEN FOSTER SONG BOOK, Stephen Foster. 40 favorites: "Beautiful Dreamer," "Camptown Races," "Jeanie with the Light Brown Hair," "My Old Kentucky Home," etc. 224pp. 9 x 12. 23048-1

"TAKE ME OUT TO THE BALL GAME" AND OTHER FAVORITE SONG HITS, 1906–1908, Lester Levy (ed.). 23 favorite songs from the turn-of-the-century with lyrics and original sheet music covers: "Cuddle Up a Little Closer, Lovey Mine," "Harrigan," "Shine on, Harvest Moon," "School Days," other hits. 128pp. 9 x 12. 24662-0

35 SONG HITS BY GREAT BLACK SONGWRITERS: Bert Williams, Eubie Blake, Ernest Hogan and Others, David A. Jasen (ed.). Ballads, show tunes, other early 20th-century works by black songwriters include "Some of These Days," "A Good Man Is Hard to Find," "I'm Just Wild About Harry," "Love Will Find a Way," 31 other classics. Reprinted from rare sheet music, original covers. 160pp. 9 x 12. (Available in U.S. only) 40416-1

Available from your music dealer or write for free Music Catalog to
Dover Publications, Inc., Dept. MUBI, 31 East 2nd Street, Mineola, NY 11501
Visit us online at www.doverpublications.com